FLIPPIN'
THE SCRIPT

by Christina Abby

In memory of Christian Alan

Introduction

The Bible is the way to eternity and preservation, so pick it up and review the Divine revelation. On the road to Damascus, St. Paul's epiphany did bring: The love of people trumps the religiosity thing. For knowing isn't a function of the head, but a byproduct of the heart that cultivates our holiness and fosters our being set apart.

Come, join me on an inward journey where lives are literally turned upside down, and where the cross at Calvary becomes our life line and crown. Where daily surrender of our will necessitates our being openminded, quiet and still. And where in and through faith, plus a focused head and heartfelt attention span, we see and embrace the Divine and His more greater plan. A plan where, indisputably, wisdom is the combination of head and heart — the two: designed to define and shape our destiny, and instruct us in what to say and do.

Come, come let us gather in this inviting place simply called Amazing Grace. The spot and space where, eucharistically, Flippin' The Script makes our journey a pleasantly wonderful trip!

I will stand upon my watch, and set me upon the tower,
and will watch to see what he will say unto me, and what
I shall answer when I am reproved. And the Lord answered
me, and said, Write the vision, and make it plain upon
tables, that he may run that read it. For the vision is yet
for an appointed time, but at the end it shall speak, and
not lie: though it tarry, wait for it; because it will surely
come, it will not tarry. Behold, his soul which is lifted up
is not upright in him: but the just shall live by his faith.

Habakkuk 2:1, 2, 3, 4

9/9/2013

To my
Dearest Sister

I dedicate this
book to our pure sisterhood.

I love you and
wish you everything your
heart desires and your faith

Can See

Your Girl
Alexia
Sisters forever
I Love
you

In Genesis the world was made,
In Exodus the march was told;
Leviticus contains the law,
In Numbers are the tribes enrolled;

In Deuteronomy again
We're urged to keep God's law alone.
And these five books of Moses make
The oldest writings that are known

Brave Joshua to Canaan leads,
In Judges oft the Jews rebel;
We read of David's name in Ruth,
And First and Second Samuel;

In First and Second Kings we read
How bad the Hebrew state became;
In First and Second Chronicles,
Another history of the same.

In Ezra captive Jews return,
While Nehemiah builds the wall;
Queen Esther saves her race from death.
These books "Historical" we call.

In Job we read of patient faith
The Psalms are David's songs of praise;
The Proverbs are to make us wise;
Eccelesiastes next portrays

How vain fleeting earthly pleasures are;
The Song of Solomon is all
About the love of God, and these
Five books "Poetical" we call

Isaiah tells of Christ to come,
And in his Lamentations mourns
The Holy City's overthrow.
Ezekiel speaks of mysteries,
While Daniel foretells kings of old;
Hoesea calls men to repent;
In Joel, judgments are foretold.

Amos tells of wrath, and Edom
Obadiah is sent to warn,
While Jonah shows how Christ should rise,
And Micah where He should be born;

In Nahum, Nineveh is seen,
In Habakkuk, Chaldea's guilt
Zephaniah, Judah's sins
In Haggai, the temple's built.

Zechariah tells of Christ,
And Malachi of John, his signs.
The Prophets number seventeen,
And all the books are thirty-nine.

Matthew, Mark, Luke and John
Tell of Christ, His life they trace;

Acts shows the Holy Spirit's work;
And Romans how we're saved by grace.

Corinthians instructs the church,
Galatians shows God's grace alone;
Ephesians, how we are "in Christ,"
Phillipians, Christ's joys make known.

Colossians portrays Christ exalted.
And Thessalonians tells the end.
In Timothy and Titus both,
Are rules for pastors to attend.

Philemon pictures charity,
Thirteen Epistles, penned by Paul
The Jewish law prefigured Christ;
And Hebrews clearly shows it all.

James shows that faith by works must live,
And Peter urges steadfastness,
While John exhorts to Christian love;
And those who live it, God will bless.

Jude shows the end of evil men,
While Revelation tells of heaven
These end the whole New Testament
In all, they number twenty-seven.

Dr. Henrietta C. Mears
What The Bible Is All About

January 1

And they said one to another, Behold, this dreamer cometh. Come now therefore, and let us slay him, and cast him into some pit, and we will say, some evil beast hath devoured him: and we shall see what will become of his dreams.

Genesis 37:19, 20

Don't intend to come across arrogantly
So pardon my being so bold
BUT favor is favor is favor
And that's just how HE rolls

And Joseph's master took him, and put him into the prison, a place where the king's prisoners were bound: and he was there in the prison. But the Lord was with Joseph, and shewed him mercy, and gave him favour in the sight of the keeper of the prison.

Genesis 39:20, 21

Dreams deferred, delayed are not dreams discarded or denied.

January 2

The thief cometh not, but for to steal and, to
destroy; I am come that they might have life,
and they might have it more abundantly.

Speak Truth to power
Refuse to perpetuate the great big lie
Now is the time to undress the emperor
Not in the sweet by and by

Come unto me all ye that labor and are heavy laden and I
will give you rest. Take my yoke upon you and learn of me,
for I am meek and lowly in heart, and ye shall find rest for
your souls. For my yoke is easy and my burden is light.

Matthew 11: 28, 29, 30

Occupy and let him who stole steal no more.

January 3

And Jesus said unto him, Verily I say unto thee,
today shalt thou be with me in paradise.

Luke 23:43

Quite an unimaginable scene
An image of love at it greatest power
The King of Kings serving humankind
While meeting His maker in that horrific hour

Greater love hath no man than this that a
man lay down his life for his friends.

John 15:13

Jesus loves me this I know.

January 4

And be not conformed to this world; but be ye transformed
by the renewing of your mind, that ye may prove what
is that good, and acceptable, and perfect will of God.

Romans 12:2

Mindfulness is important and relevant
So buck the status quo
The Enemy's tricks aren't original, but predictable
When you know Him like you know you know

Thou wilt keep him in perfect peace whose mind
is stayed on thee: because he trusteth in thee.

Isaiah 26:3

The main thing is to keep the main thing the main thing
in mind.

January 5

He must increase, but I must decrease.

John 3:30

Surrender all you have and want
Exponentially you'll grow in grace
Self-sufficiency is not a viable option
We need the Spirit to run our race

Verily, verily, I say unto you, Except a corn of
wheat fall into the ground and die, it abideth alone,
but if it die, it bringeth forth much fruit.

John 12:24

Individualism is a very, very close relative of atheism.

January 6

O death where is thy sting? O grave where is thy victory?

1 Corinthians 15:55

Try not focusing on spilled milk
Why drink out of the plate instead of the cup
Our victory is an imminent reality
And the Enemy can't really muck it up

When Jesus therefore had received the vinegar, he said, It is finished: and he bowed his head, and gave up the ghost.

John 19:30

Don't be had. Don't be hoodwinked. Don't be bamboozled.

Hear, O Israel: The Lord our God is one Lord.

Deuteronomy 6:4

What you call doing
I call done
When you say many
I say One

There is one body, and one Spirit, even as ye are
called in one hope of your calling: One Lord, one
faith, one baptism, One God and Father of all, who
is above all, and through all and in you all.

Ephesians 4: 4, 5, 6

It is finished!

January 8

So then faith cometh by hearing, and
hearing by the word of God.

Romans 10:17

Believe not everything you see
Nor internalize all you hear
Our eyes and ears may deceive us
And the contradictions will immobilize and promote fear

And Peter answered him and said, Lord if it be thou,
bid me come unto thee on the water. And he said,
Come. And when Peter was come down out of the
ship, he walked on the water to go to Jesus.

Matthew 14:28, 29

It is well. It is well because Truth always prevails.

Take away the dross from the silver, and there
shall come forth a vessel for the finer.

Proverbs 25:4

Pride cometh before a fall
Something a wounded soul can never see
Sometimes the healing isn't for our perceived enemies
But the balm might be designed for you or me

And ye have forgotten the exhortation which speaketh
unto you as unto children. My son, despise not thou
the chastening of the Lord, nor faint when thou art
rebuked of Him. For whom the Lord loveth He chasteneth, and scourgeth every son whom He receiveth.

Hebrews 12:5, 6

Pain is profitable because it has purpose. In that purpose, we
find our passion. In our passion therein are our promises. In the
promises lies His power. And in His power is our provision.

January 10

And God said, Let there be light, and there was light.

Genesis 1:3

LET is an eternal operative word
That signifies openness to God's will and way
The Spirit is always willing and ready to manifest itself
Wherever we go, and in whatever we do and say

Let the words of my mouth, and the meditation of my heart be
acceptable in thy sight, O Lord, my strength and my redeemer.

Psalms 19:14

Permission commands His Presence.

But a certain man named Ananias, with Sapphira
his wife sold a possession. And kept back part of the
price, his wife also being privy to it, and brought
a certain part and laid it at the apostles' feet.

Acts 5: 1, 2

It may be hidden temporarily
But without wavering and without a doubt
Light will overshadow our darkness
Thus, our sins will eventually find us out

But if ye will not do so, behold, ye have sinned against the
Lord, and before Israel; and be sure your sin will find you out.

Numbers 32:23

Can a man rob God?

January 12

Be sober, be vigilant; because your adversary the devil, as a roaring lion, walketh about seeking whom he may devour.

Judge not according to appearances
No need to be overly uptight
The lion's teeth have been taken away
So his roar is much bigger than his bite

Say ye not, A confederacy, to all them to whom this people shall say, A confederacy, neither fear ye their fear, nor be afraid. Sanctify the Lord of hosts himself and let him be your fear, and let him be your dread.

Isaiah 8:12, 13

FEAR: False Evidence Appearing Real.

And when they had fulfilled all that was written of him, they took him down from the tree, and laid him in a sepulcher. But God raised him from the dead.

Acts 13:29, 30

He did die
BUT yet He arose
Read for yourself
Its not written in prose

Blessed is the man that walketh not in the counsel of the ungodly nor standeth in the way of sinners, nor sitteth in the seat of the scornful. But his delight is in the law of the Lord, and in his law doth he meditate day and night.

Psalm 1: 1, 2

BUT is a small conjunction that serves a tremendous function.

January 14

Blessed are they which are persecuted for righteousness
sake, for theirs is the kingdom of heaven. Blessed are ye
when men shall revile you and persecute you, and shall say
all manner of evil against you falsely for my sake. Rejoice,
and be exceeding glad for great is your reward in heaven for
so persecuted they the prophets which were before you.

Matthew 5:10, 11, 12

What you call a curse
I call a blessing
What you call conforming
I call digressing

And be not conformed to this world, but be ye transformed
by the renewing of your mind that ye may prove what
is that good, and acceptable, and perfect will of God.

Romans 12:2

Our transformation process is progressive and hardly peaceful,
palatable, or pretty.

January 15

Hope deferred maketh the heart sick, but when
the desire cometh, it is a tree of life.

Proverbs 13:12

Dreams deferred are not necessarily denied
But are often placed on hold
Preparation is a prerequisite to manifestation
So in our patience possess our souls

And Joseph said unto them, Fear not; for am I in
the place of God? But as for you, ye thought evil
against me; but God meant it unto good to bring to
pass, as it is this day, to save much people alive.

Genesis 50:19, 20

The caterpillar had almost given up; THEN, he turned into
a butterfly.

January 16

For this thing I besought the Lord thrice that it might depart from me. And he said unto me, My grace is sufficient for thee; for my strength is made perfect in weakness. Most gladly therefore will I rather glory in my infirmities, that the power of Christ may rest upon me.

2 Corinthians 12:8, 9

Challenges and temptations are facts of life
Unconquerable in our own strength
Reflect back on the myriad conundrums you've found yourself
And remember they came and went

There hath no temptation taken you but such as is common to man; but God is faithful, who will not suffer you to be tempted above that ye are able; but will with the temptation also make a way to escape, that ye may be able to bear it.

1 Corinthians 10:13

Aren't you glad that trouble doesn't last always?

January 17

Pray without ceasing.

1 Thessalonians 5:17

Be observant and always pray
Trouble can and will cascade
Before we can wrap our minds around the happenings
We've engaged ourselves in a fruitless escapade

Confess your faults one to another, and pray for
one another, that ye may be healed. The effectual
fervent prayer of a righteous man availeth much.

James 5:16

What you don't address will ultimately cause you stress.

January 18

And the Lord said unto Satan, Hast thou considered my servant Job, that there is none like him in the
earth, a perfect and an upright man, one that feareth
God and escheweth evil? Then Satan answered the
Lord, and said, Doth Job fear God for nought?

Job 1:8, 9

Before the foundation of the world
Every detail was planned and He took a rest
The Enemy can't penetrate our hedge without permission
So situations and circumstances are only allowed at God's behest

Hast not thou made a hedge about him, and about his house,
and about all that he hath on every side? Thou hast blessed the
work of his hands, and his substance is increased in the land. But
put forth thine hand now, and touch all that he hath, and he will
curse thee in thy face. And the Lord said unto Satan, Behold,
all that hath is in thy power, only upon himself put not forth
thine hand. So Satan went forth from the presence of the Lord.

Job 1:10, 11, 12

Inconvenient truths are the most revelatory.

January 19

When wisdom entereth into thine heart, and knowledge is pleasant unto thy soul; Discretion shall preserve thee, understanding shall keep thee.

Proverbs 2:10, 11

Wisdom is the principal thing
Ask also for understanding and direction
Listen to and follow the guidance given
Then fear not nor worry about your protection

I will bless the Lord who hath given me counsel: my reins also
instruct me in the night seasons. I have set the Lord always
before me; because he is at my right hand, I shall not be moved.

Psalm 16:7, 8

Knowledge is the understanding that helps you make the peanut
butter and bread. Wisdom is the instrument that helps you apply
the spread.

January 20

And he said unto them, I beheld Satan
as lightning fall from heaven.

Luke 10:18

The Enemy is a bully
So give him no slack
Appropriate every tittle of Truth you know
And watch the Empire strike back

And you shall know the truth, and the truth shall make you free.

John 8:32

The Enemy's tricks are old as prostitution.

Though I speak with the tongues of men and angels, and have
not charity, I am become a sounding brass, or a tinkling cymbal.

1 Corinthians 13:1

When you say hatred
I say love
When you below
I say above

Set your affection on things above, not on things on the earth.

Colossians 3:2

Love is the higher road that cultivates and never decimates.

January 22

Thou he slay me, yet will I trust in him; but I will maintain
mine own ways before him. He also shall be my salvation, for an hypocrite shall not come before him.

Job 13:15, 16

Will you remain faithful?
When your world is literally falling apart
That's the time to dig your heels down deeper
And trust with all your strength, mind, and heart

And Moses said unto the people, Fear ye not, stand still
and see the salvation of the Lord, which he will shew
to you today; for the Egyptians whom ye have seen
today, ye shall see them again no more forever. The Lord
shall fight for you, and ye shall hold your peace.

Exodus 14:13, 14

Our personal limitations should foster our spiritual liberation.

January 23

The fear of the Lord is to hate evil: pride and arrogancy,
and the evil way, and the froward mouth do I hate.

Proverbs 8:13

What is man?
He who thinks he knows everything doesn't really know
He knows that there's nothing more humiliating
Than the deflation of his ego

But he giveth more grace. Wherefore he saith, God
resisteth the proud, but giveth grace unto the humble.

James 4:6

The higher the monkey climbs, the easier it is to see his butt.

January 24

For our light affliction, which is but for a moment, worketh for us a far more exceedingly and eternal weight of glory. While we look not at the things which are seen, for the things which are seen are temporal; but the things which are not seen are eternal.

2 Corinthians 4:17, 18

Cleanliness is next to godliness
But removal of the grime is gonna hurt
God loves us too much to leave us in our filth
So He meticulously disintegrates the dirt

For his anger endureth but a moment; in his favour is life: weeping may endure for a night, but joy comes in the morning.

Psalms 30:5

From hurt to hallelujah, my soul is a witness.

January 25

Be strong and of a good courage, fear not, nor be afraid
of them: for the Lord thy God, he it is that doth go
with thee; he will not fail thee, nor forsake thee.

Deuteronomy 31:6

In confusion, discouragement, and dismay
The liars start making sense
Don't believe the Enemy's hissing and hype
Truth and Truth alone is our greatest defense

Fear thou not for I am with thee; be not dismayed; for I am
thy God. I will strengthen thee; yea, I will help thee; yea I
will uphold thee with the right hand of my righteousness.

Isaiah 41:10

Flip the Script and let the Word do the work.

January 26

Forever, O Lord, thy word is settled in heaven.

Psalm 119:89

Dark, stormy clouds rising
Ship Ahoy! Ship Ahoy!
The Word is the anchor of our souls
The essence and center of our joy

Then he said unto them, Go your way, eat the fat, and drink
the sweet, and send portions unto them for whom nothing
is prepared: for this day is holy unto our Lord; neither
be ye sorry; for the joy of the Lord is your strength.

Nehemiah 8:10

Your Word is a lamp to my path and the peace in my storms.

January 27

Now the parable is this: The seed is the word of God.

There is no variation or partiality
The message of old still rings true
There's a cloud of witnesses to its veracity
What He did for others, He's still doing for me and you

And all things are of God, who hath reconciled us to himself by Jesus Christ, and hath given to us the ministry of reconciliation. To wit, that God was in Christ, reconciling the world unto himself, not imputing their trespasses unto them; and hath committed unto us the word of reconciliation.

2 Corinthians 5:18, 19

Reconciliation of the seemingly opposites is the springboard to Christ-consciousness.

Behold, I send you forth as sheep in the midst of wolves;
be ye therefore wise as serpents, and harmless as doves.

Matthew 10:16

When you say in
I say out
What you call disenfranchisement
I call clout

As sorrowful, yet always rejoicing, as poor, yet making many
rich, as having nothing, and yet possessing all things.

2 Corinthians 6:10

Service supersedes self and principle triumphs personality.

January 29

A double-minded man is unstable in all of his ways.

Being tossed to and fro?
The key is to master the art of being steady
Knowing that the unchangeable is changeless
And a Christ-centered mind is the sign of your being ready

Thou believest that there is one God; thou doest
well; devils also believe, and tremble.

James 1:19

Change your thinking and change your life.

Flippin The Script | 29

January 30

For as a man thinketh in his heart, so is he.

Proverbs 23:7

Leave no vacancy for negativity
So guard your heart and mind
Our predominant thoughts will be amplified
And reproduce themselves seven times seven their kind

Finally, brethren, whatsoever things are true, whatsoever
things are honest, whatsoever things are just, whatsoever
things are pure, whatsoever things are lovely, whatsoever things are of a good report; if there be any virtue,
and if there be any praise, think on these things.

Philippians 4:8

I think you and I are divine.

I beseech you therefore, brethren, by the mercies of
God, that you present your bodies a living sacrifice, holy,
acceptable to God, which is your reasonable service.

Romans 12:1

Consecration is our lofty goal
With a conscientious removal of stain and dross
Like teeth need a cleaning solution and apparatus
Our stinking thinking requires mental floss

For you were bought at a price; therefore glorify God
in your body and in your spirit, which are God's.

1 Corinthians 6:20

I owe. I owe. I owe so back to my God I go.

February 1

Then Jezebel sent a messenger to Elijah saying, So let the gods do to me, and more also, if I do not make your life as the life of one of them by tomorrow about this time. And when he saw that, he arose and ran for his life, and went to Beersheba, which belongs to Judea and left his servant there.

1 Kings 19: 2, 3

Fear stagnates and paralyzes
And may create trauma that we may be unable to bear
But others can't float our balloon unless we let them
For our individual destiny is not based on another's hot air

And Elijah came to all the people and said, How long will you falter between two opinions? If the Lord is God, follow Him; but if Baal, follow him. But the people answered him not a word.

1 Kings 18:21

Remember: The stone that the builders rejected became the chief cornerstone.

February 2

Many are the afflictions of the righteous but
the Lord delivers them out of them all.

Psalm 34:19

Struggles and disappointments are inevitable
Just keep hold of His unchanging hand
We'll never ever be alone
He'll incorporate everything into His master plan

And we know that all things work together for
the good to them that love God, to them who
are the called according to his purpose.

Romans 8:28

Nothing is ever wasted: A curse becomes a blessing in disguise.

February 3

For all the promises of God in him are yea, and
in him Amen, unto the glory of God by us.

2 Corinthians 1:20

Our provision lies in His promises
Individually, collectively there's many for you and me
But our loose lips can sink our ships
And detour our progression toward where we're supposed to be

For thus saith the Lord God, the Holy One of Israel: In
returning and rest shall ye be saved; in quietness and in
confidence shall be your strength: and ye would not.

Isaiah 30:15

The exotic fish wouldn't have gotten caught if he had just kept
his mouth shut.

February 4

He that passeth by, and meddleth with strife belonging
not to him, is like one that taketh a dog by the ears.

Proverbs 26:17

Carefully choose your battles
Every discord and disagreement is not worth a fight
If they're no spoils to be obtained afterwards
Then it really doesn't matter who's wrong or right

For we hear that there are some which walk among you
disorderly, working not at all, but are busybodies.

2 Thessalonians 3:11

Being right isn't necessarily righteous.

February 5

Fear not I am with you, be not dismayed for I am
your God. I will strengthen you, yes I will help you.
I will withhold you with my righteous hand.

Isaiah 41:10

Dump all of your burdens at the altar
He knows all about them and is willing to share
Remember, no tear is ever lost or wasted
When our concerns are placed in the Master's care

He that goeth forth and weepeth, bearing precious seed, shall doubtless come again with rejoicing, bringing his sheaves with him.

Psalm 126:6

We'd never know that He's a problem solver if we never had
any problems.

February 6

Before I formed thee in the belly I knew thee; and
before thou camest forth out of the womb I sanctified
thee, and I ordained thee a prophet unto the nations.

Jeremiah 1:5

Be authentic. Be for real
There's no need trying to pretend
For pretentiousness springs from a root of ignorance
He knows our core; our beginning and end

You have not chosen me, but I have chosen you, and
ordained you, that ye should go and bring forth fruit,
and that your fruit should remain: that whatsoever ye
shall ask the Father in my name, he may give it you.

John 15:16

The true you is always better than a fake somebody else.

February 7

If my people, which are called by name shall humble
themselves, and pray, and seek my face, and turn from
their wicked ways, then I will hear from heaven, and
will forgive their sin, and will heal their land.

2 Chronicles 7:14

What you call pain
I call healing
What you think is hidden
I think and know to be revealing

So shall my word be that goeth forth out of my mouth. It shall
not return unto me void, but it shall accomplish that which
I please, and it shall prosper in the thing whereto I sent it.

Isaiah 55:11

Just because we can't see it coming doesn't mean that it is not
on its way.

February 8

To every thing there is as season, and a time
to every purpose under the heaven.

Everything and everybody has purpose
That's revealed at a specific season or time
Nothing is random but divinely ordered
Given direction, the world can stop on a dime

I form the light and create darkness. I make war and
create peace. I the Lord do all these things.

Isaiah 45:7

He spoke and it was done.

Flippin The Script | 39

February 9

Where wast thou when I laid the foundations of
the earth? Declare, if thou hast understanding. Who
hath laid the measures thereof, if thou knowest?
Or who hath stretched the line upon it?

Job 38: 4, 5

This King has a real kingdom
Not just your ordinary run of the mill
He erects, directs and maintains universal order
And owns the cattle on a thousand hills

All things were created through Him and for Him.

Colossians 1:18

What a mighty God we serve.

February 10

Behold, I will do a new thing; now it shall spring
forth shall ye not know it? I will even make a way
in the wilderness, and rivers in the desert.

Isaiah 43:19

Transformative change is difficult
But the end results are worth our try
For solving the problem without effort is rather delusional
Like knowing the Truth and still believing the lie

And no one pours new wine into old wineskins. If he
does, the new wine will burst the skins, the wine will run
out and the wineskins will be ruined. No, new wine must
be poured into new wineskins. And no one after drinking
old wine wants the new, the he says, The old is better.

Luke 5: 37, 38, 39

Familiarity can be absolutely fatal.

February 11

Ho, every one that thirsteth, come ye to the waters, and
he that hath no money, come ye, buy and eat; yea, come,
buy wine and milk without money and without price.

Isaiah 55:1

Salvation is a precious gift
That has never been for sale
We can attend and give everything we have to the church
And still not be spiritually well

My sheep hear my voice, and I know them, and they follow
me. And I give them eternal life; and they shall never perish,
neither shall any man pluck them out of my hand.

John 10: 27, 28

Relationship and not religion is the answer to the riddle.

Truth shall spring up from the earth and righteous shall look down from heaven.

Psalm 85:11

Truth understood
Does not waver or bend
Our resurrection always comes
At our perceived dead end

Now when He had said these things, He cried with a loud voice, Lazarus, come forth! And he who had died came out bound hand foot with graveclothes, and his face was wrapped with a cloth. Jesus said to them, Loose him, and let him go.

John 11: 43, 44

And you shall know the Truth and the Truth shall set you free.

February 13

And Jesus answered and said unto her, Martha, Martha,
thou art careful and troubled about many things. But
one thing is needful, and Mary hath chosen that good
part, which shall not be taken away from her.

Luke 10: 41, 42

Ritualism and religiosity are unfulfilling
And there's an important reason why
They're empty attempts to fill a void
That only true relationship can satisfy

For he satisfieth the longing soul and filleth
the hungry soul with goodness.

Psalm 107:9

Seek the King and His kingdom first and all other things will
be added.

The wolf also shall dwell with the lamb, and the leopard shall lie down with the kid, and the calf and the young lion and the fatling together, and a little child shall lead them.

Isaiah 11:6

When you say big
I say small
When you say short
I say tall

But when thou art bidden, go and sit down in the lowest room; that when he that bade thee cometh, he may say unto thee: Friend, go up higher, then shalt thou have worship in the presence of them that sit at meat with thee. For whosoever exalteth himself shall be abased, and he that humbleth himself shall be exalted.

Luke 14:10, 11

Honor is bestowed when humility is displayed.

February 15

We are troubled on every side, yet not distressed; we
are perplexed, but not in despair; persecuted, but not
forsaken; cast down, but not destroyed. Always bearing
about in the body the dying of the Lord Jesus, that the
life also of Jesus might be made manifest in our body.

2 Corinthians 4: 8, 9, 10

Disappointment can be dangerous
And may promote feelings of being accursed
But be not dismayed, but excited, in your affliction
For our circumstances can be divinely reversed

For our light affliction, which is but for a moment, worketh
for us a far more exceeding and eternal weight of glory.
While we look not at the things which are seen, but at the
things which are not seen; for the things which are seen are
temporal; but the things which are not seen are eternal.

2 Corinthians 4: 17, 18

The process is just as important as our progress.

For which of you, intending to build a tower, sitteth not down first, and counteth the cost, whether he have sufficient to finish it? Lest haply, after he hath laid the foundation, and is not able to finish it, all that behold it begin to mock him.

Luke 14: 28, 29

There's always a cost to pay
The fulfillment of promises is conditional, you see
While salvation and grace is truly amazing
Free is not all that it is cooked up to be

And he said to them all, If any man will come after me, let him deny himself, and take up his cross daily and follow me. For whosoever will save his life shall lose it; but whosoever will lose his life for my sake, the same shall save it.

Luke 9: 23, 24

His grace is sufficient and His strength and power is made perfect in our weakness.

February 17

And if it seem evil unto you to serve the Lord, choose
you this day whom ye will serve; whether the gods which
your fathers served that were on the other side of the
flood, or the gods of the Amorites, in whose land ye dwell;
but as for me and my house, we will serve the Lord.

Joshua 24:15

We may be at life's intersection
Of what we want and what we need to reject
Remember, God won't remove our needful things
And likewise our insignificants He won't resurrect

No man can serve two masters, for either he will hate the
one, and love the other; or else he will hold to the one, and
despise the other. Ye cannot serve God and mammon.

Matthew 6:24

Let the dead bury the dead and follow the road less traveled.

February 18

And when his brethren saw that their father loved him more than all his brethren, they hated him, and could not speak peaceably unto him. And Joseph dreamed a dream, and he told it his brethren: and they hated him yet the more.

Genesis 37: 4, 5

Persevere. Persevere.
You can get up, I bet
In fact, if you're reading these words
You're not quite out of the race yet

For a righteous man may fall seven times and rise again, but the wicked shall fall by calamity.

Proverbs 24:16

Still I rise. I Rise. I Rise.

February 19

Behold, I send you forth as sheep in the midst of wolves;
be ye therefore wise as serpents, and harmless as doves.

Matthew 10:16

Give the Jezebel spirit an inroad
And our progress will surely stagnate
Give her an inch, she'll take a mile
So recognize her but don't tolerate

And Jesus answered and said unto him, Get thee
behind me, Satan, for it is written, Thou shalt worship
the Lord thy God, and him only shalt thou serve.

Luke 4:8

Nip it in the bud before the bud begins to blossom.

February 20

For thus saith the Lord God, the Holy One of Israel; in returning and rest shall ye be saved; in quietness and in confidence shall be your strength, and ye would not.

Isaiah 30:15

Solitude is elemental to spiritual growth
For it is conducive for meditation
Beware of self-absorption during this time
For it will cause spiritual isolation

Let the words of my mouth, and the meditation of my heart, be acceptable in thy sight, O Lord, my strength, and my redeemer.

Psalm 19:14

Truth must penetrate in order to operate.

February 21

This book of the law shall not depart out of thy
mouth; but thou shall meditate therein day and night,
that thou mayest observe to do according to all that
is written therein, for then thou shalt make thy way
prosperous, and thou shall have good success.

Joshua 1:8

What you call simple
I call profound
What you call the cross
I call the crown

And, behold, the veil of the temple was rent in twain
from the top to the bottom; and the earth did quake,
and the rocks rent; And the graves were opened; and
many bodies of the saints which slept arose.

Matthew 27:51, 52

1 cross + 3 nails = 4given.

February 22

I will go before you and make the crooked places straight;
I will break in pieces the gates of bronze and cut the bars
of iron. I will give you the treasures of darkness and hidden
riches of secret places, that you may know that I, the Lord,
who call you by your name, am the God of Israel.

Isaiah 45:2, 3

May you prosper in all you do
And not just exist or survive
Declare and proclaim the promises
Dwell in them and consequently thrive

Look unto Me, and be saved, all the ends of the
earth! For I am God, and there no other.

Isaiah 45:22

Painful problems often precede our providential promises.

February 23

Then God remembered Noah, and every living thing, and
all the animals that were with him in the ark. And God
made a wind to pass over the earth, and waters subsided.

The tides are churning in our favor
The table of fruition is being readied and set
The silence you hear is not really a NO
But an assurance of YES, but NOT YET

In your patience possess your souls.

Luke 21:19

All of the promises of God are Yes and Amen.

64 | Christina Aboo

February 24

O God, how long shall the adversary reproach?
Shall the enemy blaspheme thy name forever?

Psalm 74:10

Waiting is nerve-wrecking
Annoyingly difficult to digest
Time's enemy is anxiety
While faith is our proactive, true trust test

Do not be deceived; God is not mocked; for whatsoever a man soweth, that shall he also reap.

Galatians 6:7

Recompense may be delayed. BUT, make no mistake, the Piper
always gets paid.

February 25

Can a woman forget her sucking child, that she should not have compassion on the son of her womb? Yea, they may forget, yet will I not forget thee.

Isaiah 49:15

His mercy fails not
And He never forgets
Just keep doing the good that you do
And you'll never have remorse or regrets

When he maketh inquisition for blood, he remembereth them; he forgetteth not the cry of the humble.

Psalm 9:12

Great is Thy faithfulness.

But he turned, and said unto Peter, Get thee behind me,
Satan; thou art an offence unto me; for thou savourest not
the things that be of God, but those that be of men.

Matthew 16:23

The Enemy is a sadist
And oh the dissension he conceives
When we allow him to captivate our imagination
He cloaks the lie that he wishes us to internalize and believe

He that is not with me is against me; and he that
gathereth not with me scattereth abroad.

Matthew 12:30

What a web he weaves when he successfully assures our belief in
what he conceives.

If the foundations be destroyed, what can the righteous do?

Psalm 11:3

Lightning strikes, while thunder rolls
The tempest winds assail
Our dark clouds will eventually subside
And Divine purpose will always prevail

For there is nothing covered that shall not be
revealed; neither hid that shall not be known.

Luke 12:2

The darkest hour is right before the dawn.

But what things were gain to me, those I counted loss for Christ. Yea doubtless, and I count all things but loss for the excellency of the knowledge of Christ Jesus my Lord: for whom I have suffered the loss of all things, and do count them dung, that I may win Christ.

Philippians 3:7, 8

When you say loss
I say gain
What you call sunshine
I call rain

Whosoever shall seek to save his life shall lose it; and whosoever shall lose his life shall preserve it.

Luke 15:33

Let it rain. Let it rain.

March 1

Many are the afflictions of the righteous, but
the Lord delivereth them out of them all.

Psalm 34:19

The school of hard knocks
Sometimes leads us in muckety muck
But there are valuable lessons to be learned in the mire:
First, take stock and know when you're stuck

Call unto me, and I will answer thee, and show thee
great and mighty things which thou knowest not.

Jeremiah 33:3

The things that assail us make us numb; but, we'll never get any-
where if we choose to stay stuck on stupid and parked on dumb.

March 2

Oh the depth of the riches both of the wisdom
and knowledge of God! How unsearchable are his
judgments, and his ways past finding out!

Romans 11:33

All our answers won't be apprehended
On this side of eternity
However, we know more than we think we know
But only the Creator has the master key

For I know the thoughts I think toward you, saith the Lord,
thoughts of peace, and not of evil, to give you an expected end.

Jeremiah 29:11

First the promise, then the problem; and finally the provision.

March 3

My brethren, count it all joy when ye fall into divers temptations, knowing this, that the trying of your faith worketh patience. But let patience have her perfect work, that ye may be perfect and entire, wanting nothing.

James 1: 2, 3, 4

Don't give up or in
The victory is ours, for sure
Our challenge in the midst of adversity
Quite frankly is to just endure

And not only so, but we glory in tribulations also; knowing that tribulation worketh patience; And patience, experience; and experience, hope; And hope maketh not ashamed; because the love of God is shed abroad in our hearts by the Holy Ghost which is given unto us.

Romans 5; 3, 4, 5

Triumph is within our perceived tragedy.

March 4

Death and life are in the power of the tongue; and
they that love it shall eat the fruit thereof.

Proverbs 18:21

Positivity is mysteriously powerful
So carefully choose the words you say
And know that pessimism will positively function as it should
Just say, "What I'm doing won't work anyway."

A fool uttered all his mind; but a wise
man keepeth it in till afterwards.

Proverbs 29:11

A word to the wise: Listen twice as much as you talk. That's why
God gave us two ears and one mouth.

March 5

And the high priest stood up in the midst, and asked Jesus, saying, Answerest thou nothing? What is it which these witness against thee? But he held his peace and answered nothing. Again the high priest asked him and said unto him, Art thou the Christ, the Son of the Blessed?

Mark 14:60, 61

Silence is golden
And can avert a royal mess
But what we don't address
Will ultimately cause us enormous stress

And Jesus said, I am; and ye shall see the Son of Man sitting on the right hand of power, and coming in the clouds of heaven.

Mark 14:62

Silence is thunderous BUT Truth strikes like lightning.

March 6

For if ye forgive men their trespasses, your heavenly Father
will also forgive you; But if ye forgive not men their trespasses, neither will your Father forgive your trespasses.

Matthew 6: 14, 15

Has someone betrayed you?
Quickly, get the situation under control
Forgiveness begins your healing process
A salve of benefit to your heart, mind, body and soul

Blessed is he whose transgression is forgiven, whose sin is covered.

Psalm 32:1

Keep calm and carry on.

March 7

But God raised Him from the dead.

Acts 13:30

When say tragedy
I say triumph
What you call an abyss
I call a bump

For a just man falleth seven times, and riseth up
again: but the wicked shall fall into mischief.

Proverbs 24:16

Truth shall spring up from the earth and righteous shall look
down from heaven.

March 8

Cast me not away from thy presence, and
take not thy holy spirit from me.

Psalm 51:11

There's a dark night of the soul
And if you've ever been there, you remember and know
But if you're not yet acquainted
It's a place you really don't want to be or go

I sought the Lord and he heard me and
delivered me from my fears.

Psalm 34:4

Out of the depth of our darkest hour we see the glory of His
omniscient power.

March 9

The liberal soul shall be made fat and he that
watereth shall be watered also himself.

Proverbs 11:25

Give without hesitation
And you'll never be in lack
Our return is in our investment
For reciprocation is how the Universe pays back

Give, and it shall be given unto you; good measure, pressed
down, and shaken together, and running over, shall men
give into your bosom. For with the same measure that
ye mete withal it shall be measured to you again.

Luke 6:38

Attack your lack by giving liberally of what you have back.

March 10

Enter ye in at the strait gate: for wide is the gate, and broad is the way, that leadeth to destruction, and many there be which go in there at. Because strait is the gate, and narrow is the way, which leadeth unto life, and few there be that find it.

Matthew 7:13, 14

Expect the unexpected
Barriers can be bridges to success
Focusing on the problem instead of the Presence
Impairs our thinking and impedes our access

There hath no temptation taken you but such as is common to man: but God is faithful, who will not suffer you to be tempted above that ye are able, but will with the temptation also make a way to escape, that ye may be able to bear it.

1 Corinthians 10:13

He is trustworthy; therefore, search for treasures in the trials.

March 11

Therefore if any man be in Christ, he is a new creature: old
things are passed away; behold, all things are become new.

2 Corinthians 5:17

Remember, we're brand new people
So no more entering the old, closed doors
We have to remind ourselves
That our mindsets don't reside there anymore

And be not conformed to this world; but be ye transformed
by the renewing of your mind, that ye may prove what
is that good, and acceptable, and perfect will of God.

Romans 12:2

Re-mind yourself and constantly remember.

March 12

But what things were gain to me, those
I counted loss for Christ.

When we've lost it all
Then we'll find that we already have what we really need
For, phenomenally, the beautiful, majestic oak
Is found inside of a puny acorn seed

Then said he, Unto what is the kingdom of God like?
And whereunto shall I resemble it? It is like a grain
of mustard seed, which a man took, and cast into his
garden; and it grew, and waxed a great tree; and the
fowls of the air lodged in the branches of it.

Luke 13:18, 19

Little is much when God is in it. The kingdom is within.

March 13

But a certain Samaritan, as he journeyed, came where he
was; and when he saw him, he had compassion on him.

Luke 10:33

We're blessed to glorify God
And not meant to make our own heads swell
Blessings multiply exponentially
When we wear them compassionately well

For ye are bought with a price; therefore glorify God
in your body, and in your spirit, which are God's.

1 Corinthians 6:20

It is more blessed to give than receive.

March 14

I will declare the decree, the Lord hath said unto me:
Thou art my son; this day have I begotten thee. Ask of me,
and I shall give thee the heathen for thine inheritance,
and the uttermost parts of the earth for thy possession.

Psalm 2:7, 8

When you say poor
I say rich
What you call the glamour
I call the gilded glitch

But the rich, in that he is made low, because as the flower
of the grass he shall pass away. For the sun is no sooner
risen with a burning heat, but it withered the grass, and
flower thereof falleth, and the grace of the fashion of it
perisheth: so shall the rich man fade away in his ways.

James 1:10, 11

All that glitters ain't really gold and all kinds of substance won't
satisfy the soul.

March 15

And he trembling and astonished said, Lord what wilt thou
have me to do? And the Lord said unto him, Arise, and go
into the city, and it shall be told what thou must do.

Acts 9:6

Conversion takes but a moment
But it does not remove our hardship and strife
Transformation is an ongoing process
That arrests and changes our outlook and life

But the Lord said unto him, Go thy way: for he is a chosen
vessel unto me, to bear my name before the Gentiles,
and kings and the children of Israel: For I will shew him
how great things he must suffer for my name's sake.

Acts 9:15, 16

Some of the most beautiful flowers grow in the largest and most
putrid piles of manure.

March 16

Turn again, and tell Hezekiah the captain of my people, Thus saith the Lord, the God of David thy father, I have heard thy prayer, I have seen thy tears: behold, I will heal thee: on the third day thou shalt go up unto the house of the Lord. And I will add unto thy days fifteen years; and I will deliver thee and this city out of the hand of the king of Assyria; and I will defend this city for mine own sake, and for my servant David's sake.

2 Kings 20:5, 6

I once was lost
And now I'm found
I should have been dead
But I'm still above ground

And he said unto me, My grace is sufficient for thee: for my strength is made perfect in weakness. Most gladly therefore will I rather glory in my infirmities, that the power of Christ may rest upon me.

2 Corinthians 12:9

Amazing grace, how sweet the sound.........

March 17

As it written, There is none that is righteous, not one.

Romans 3:12

Christianity is powerfully dynamic
Places and things come and go as they may
But what is man going to do
When his prim, props, and pretentions suddenly fall away?

Take away the dross from the silver, and there
shall come forth a vessel for the refiner.

Proverbs 25:4

The Philosopher's stone slices and dices right down to the bone.

March 18

Commit thy works unto the Lord, and
thy thoughts shall be established.

Proverbs 16:3

Circumstances can be less than optimal
But we can rise out of the mold and mire
The Mind's eye is quite perceptive
In shaping the vision of the heart's desire

Delight thyself also in the Lord; and he shall
give thee the desires of thine heart.

Psalm 37:4

In the Mind's eye is the answer to who, what, when, how, where
and why.

But he was wounded for our transgressions, he was
bruised for our iniquities; the chastisement of our peace
was upon him; and with his stripes we are healed.

Isaiah 53:5

Justified by faith
Through His righteousness not yours or mine
An incredibly expensive gift made available to all
And we'll never have to pay a dime

No weapon that is formed against thee shall prosper; and
every tongue that shall rise against thee in judgment thou
shalt condemn. This is the heritage of the servants of the
Lord, and their righteousness is of me, saith the Lord.

Isaiah 54:17

Jesus is the gift that just keeps on giving.

March 20

Arise, go to Nineveh, that great city, and cry against it; for
their wickedness is come up before me. But Jonah rose up
to flee unto Tar-shish from the presence of the Lord, and
went down to Joppa; and he found a ship going to Tar-shish;
so he paid the faire thereof, and went down into it, to go
with them unto Tar-shish from the presence of the Lord.

Jonah 1:2, 3

There's no aborting the plan of God
Many try, but with no success
Because every knee shall bow
And every tongue shall confess

Now the Lord had prepared a great fish to swallow up
Jonah. And Jonah was in the belly of the fish three days
and three nights. Then Jonah prayed unto the Lord his
God out of the fish's belly. And said, I cried by reason of
mine affliction unto the Lord, and he heard me; out of
the belly of hell cried I, and thou heardest my voice.

Jonah 1:17; 2:1, 2

Resistance is futile.

March 21

But Peter and John answered and said unto them,
whether it be right in the sight of God to hearken unto
you more than unto God, judge ye. For we cannot but
speak the things which we have seen and heard.

Acts 4:19, 20

When you say wait
I say go
When you say it isn't
I say it tis' so

And there were four leprous men at the entering in of
the gate: and they said one to another, Why sit here until
we die? If we say, We will enter into the city, then the
famine is in the city, and we shall die there; and if we
sit still here, we die also. Now therefore come, and let
us fall unto the host of the Syrians: if they save us alive,
we shall live; and if they kill us, we shall but die.

2 Kings 7:3, 4

If you don't let your past die, it won't let you live in your present
nor see into your future.

March 22

For the Son of man is come to seek and
to save that which was lost.

Some paths are less than desirable
Others take will power and sheer nerve
Not all losses are equal
But all are saved to serve

The disciple is not above his master, nor
the servant above his lord.

Matthew 10:24

Each one should reach one.

Flippin The Script | 91

March 23

There is therefore now no condemnation to them which are in Christ Jesus, who walk not after the flesh, but after the Spirit.

Romans 8:1

From sinner to Son
With no condemnation
From individual to corporate
Without hesitancy or separation

And they twain shall be one flesh; so they are no more twain, but one flesh. What therefore God hath joined together let no man put asunder.

Mark 10:8, 9

Religiosity breeds separation while spirituality achieves unification.

March 24

So that contrariwise ye ought rather to forgive him,
and comfort him, lest perhaps such a one should
be swallowed up with overmuch sorrow.

2 Corinthians 2:7

The world's in a fallen state
And daily we tread through the sludge
Overlooking the trespasses
For burdens are borne by those who hold a grudge

Judge not, and ye shall not be judged; condemn not, and ye
shall not be condemned; forgive, and ye shall be forgiven.

Luke 6:37

Unforgiveness is like drinking poison and expecting the Enemy
to die.

March 25

Now the Lord is that Spirit; and where the
Spirit of the Lord is, there is liberty.

2 Corinthians 3:17

Take hold of your liberty
Simple but profound advice
For He died a criminal's death for our freedom
How can we repay or comprehend such love and sacrifice

But God commendeth his love toward us, in that,
while we were yet sinners, Christ died for us.

Romans 5:8

At the cross, at the cross where I first saw the light.

As soon as Jesus heard the word that was spoken, he saith unto the ruler of the synagogue, Be not afraid, only believe.

Mark 5:36

You might not know where
And you may not know how
Still stand still and see your salvation
And, above all, don't dare bend or bow

For what saith the scripture? Abraham believed God, and it was counted unto him for righteousness.

Romans 4:3

He sat down so that we could stand up.

March 27

Death and life are in the power of the tongue; and
they that love it shall eat the fruit thereof.

Proverbs 18:21

Words can kill, steal or heal
For there is creativity in whatever we think, do, and say
Therefore a change in our thoughts and language
Can keep unwanted manifestations away

He sent his word, and healed them, and delivered them from their destructions.

Psalm 107:20

We've got it down pat when we're persecuted and still can wear
the white hat.

March 28

Then shall they call upon me, but I will not answer;
they shall seek me early, but they shall not find me.

Proverbs 1:28

When you say early
I say late
When you say go
I say wait

These wait all upon thee; that thou mayest
give them their meat in due season.

Psalm 104:27

The soul will remain aimlessly restless until it finds its way back
to the Father's house.

Beware of the false prophets, which come to you in
sheep's clothing, but inwardly they are ravenous wolves.

Matthew 7:15

The day has long evolved
And the night is far spent
Many preachers are called
BUT some just went!

Woe be unto the pastors that destroy and scatter the sheep of
my pasture! Therefore thus saith the Lord God Israel against
the pastors that feed my people; Ye have scattered my flock,
and driven them away, and have not visited them; behold, I
will visit upon you the evil of your doings, saith the Lord.

Jeremiah 23:1, 2

Just because the shingle says soul food doesn't mean the cooking
is any good.

March 30

For I know the thoughts that I think toward you, saith the Lord;
thoughts of peace and not of evil to give you an expected end.

Jeremiah 29:11

Afterwards, the harvest is plenteous
With more than enough to survive
I now declare prosperity in all you do
And may you both enjoy and thrive

I will go before thee, and make the crooked places straight: I
will break in pieces the gates of brass, and cut in sunder the
bars of iron. And I will give thee the treasures of darkness, and
hidden riches of secret places, that thou mayest know that I,
the Lord, which call thee by thy name, am the God of Israel.

Isaiah 45:2, 3

And your latter day shall be greater than your former.

March 31

For the weapons of our warfare are not carnal, but mighty
through God to the pulling down of strongholds. Casting
down imaginations, and every high thing that exalteth
itself against the knowledge of God, and bringing into
captivity every thought to the obedience of God.

2 Corinthians 10:4, 5

While the battle is raging
Disengagement is extremely hard
But in quietness and confidence is our strength
Our God is a warring God

And in that day thou shalt say, O Lord, I will praise thee;
thou wast angry with me, thine anger is turned away,
and thou comfortedst me. Behold, God is my salvation;
I will trust, and not be afraid: for the Lord Jehovah is my
strength and my song; he also is become my salvation.

Isaiah 12:2, 3

Our victories are in and of Him and not in or of ourselves.

April 1

And he wept aloud: and the Egyptians
and the house of Pharoah heard.

Genesis 45:2

Circumstances have you under water?
Can't seem to stay afloat
Trust that the current is changing for the better
Grab hold of the anchor and stay in the boat

And Joseph said unto his brethren, I am Joseph; doth my
father yet live? And his brethren could not answer him;
for they were troubled at his presence. Now therefore be
not grieved, nor angry with yourselves, that ye sold me
hither, for God did send me before you to preserve life.

Genesis 45:3, 5

The Captain has it all under control and will prosper and preserve the longing soul.

April 2

And the Lord said unto Satan, Whence comest thou? Then
Satan answered the Lord, and said, From going to and fro
in the earth and from walking up and down in it. And the
Lord said unto Satan, Hast thou considered my servant
Job, that there is none like him in the earth, a perfect and
upright man, one that feareth God, and escheweth evil?

Job 1:7, 8

The natural mind doesn't have the answers
As to why things happen this or that way
But the Spirit, the mind of Christ, is omniscient
So be encouraged, trust, and obey

Thou he slay me, yet will I trust in him: but I
will maintain mine own ways before him.

Job 13:15

Our most prized blessings are often wrapped in our most difficult lessons.

April 3

Now faith is the substance of things hoped
for, the evidence of things not seen.

Hebrews 11:1

Don't believe all you see
Nor internalize all you hear
Seeing is often the enemy of believing
And hearing almost always conjures up fear

So then faith cometh by hearing, and
hearing by the word of God.

Romans 10:17

Flip the Script and let the Word do the work.

April 4

Wherefore they came again, and told him. And he said,
This is the word of the Lord, which he spake by his servant
Elijah the Tishbite, saying in the portion of Jezebel shall
dogs eat the flesh of Jezebel. And the carcass of Jeebel
shall be as dung upon the face of the field in the portion
of Jezreel; so that they shall not say, This is Jezebel.

2 Kings 9:36, 37

We're responsible for our own actions
No one else is to blame
Our irresponsibility is ours to own
Equally, so do consequences belong the same

Then Judas, which had betrayed him, when he saw
that he was condemned, repented himself, and brought
again the thirty pieces of silver to the chief priests and
elders. And he cast down the pieces of silver in the
temple and departed and went and hanged himself.

Matthew 27:3, 5

Inexcusable excuses, like rusty nails, hold structures together that
are bound to fail.

April 5

Confidence in an unfaithful man in time of trouble
is like a broken tooth and a foot out of joint.

Proverbs 25:19

Some relationships are irreparably broken
Opportunities have long past to mend
Reconciliation is now just a pipe dream
Like scattering valuable time and energy in the wind

He that handleth a matter wisely shall find good;
and whoso trusteth in the Lord happy is he.

Proverbs 16:20

You have to be aware and know when its time to forget it and
let go.

April 6

And Jesus said unto him, Verily I say unto thee,
Today shalt thou be with me in paradise.

Erase the frown
And paint on a smile
TODAY is good news
Even if we have to wait a while

He that hath an ear, let him hear what the Spirit saith
unto the churches; To him that overcometh will I
give to eat of the hidden manna, and will give him
a white stone, and in the stone a new name written,
which no man knoweth saving he that receiveth it.

Revelation 2:17

An open mind has a room with a view and an open heart allows
His glory to shine through.

April 7

Now no chastening for the present seemeth to be joyous, but grievous; nevertheless afterward it yieldeth the peaceable fruit of righteousness unto them which are exercised thereby.

Hebrews 12:11

When you say pain
I say healing
What you think is hidden
I think and know to be revealing

The law of the Lord is perfect converting the soul; the testimony of the Lord is sure, making wise the simple.

Psalm 19:7

I was reborn when I was broken.

April 8

When wisdom entereth into thine heart, and knowledge is pleasant unto the soul; Discretion shall preserve thee, understanding shall keep thee.

Proverbs 2:10, 11

Consult both head and heart
For wisdom is a combo of the two
Too much head is sometimes counterproductive
And excessive altruism is not good for the benefactor or you

Many will entreat the favor of the prince; and
every man is a friend of him that giveth gifts.

Proverbs 19:6

Wisdom is what wisdom does.

April 9

Thou wilt keep him in perfect peace whose mind
is stayed on thee because he trusteth in thee.

Isaiah 26:3

Our freedom can begin today
No delay until tomorrow
For there aren't any prisoners in heaven
Neither is there pain or sorrow

And God shall wipe away all tears from their eyes; and there
shall be no more death, neither sorrow, nor crying , neither shall
there be any more pain; for the formers things are passed away.

Revelation 21:4

Free your mind and your body and soul will follow.

April 10

For now we see through a glass, darkly; but
then face to face; now I know in part; but then
shall I know even as also I am known.

1 Corinthians 13:12

It just doesn't make sense
How we get in various spots
We won't understand the particulars until later
Because He's God and we're not

So shall my word be that goeth forth out of my mouth; it shall
not return unto me void, but it shall accomplish that which
I please, and it shall prosper in the thing whereto I sent it.

Isaiah 55:11

Find and seek but don't give much credence to what your own
voice of knowledge speaks.

Then Pharoah sent and called Joseph, and they brought
him hastily out of the dungeon: and he shaved himself,
and changed his raiment, and came in unto Pharoah.

Genesis 41:14

Meanwhile, do what you have to do
To survive and make the ends meet
The Enemy might stymie progress
But destroying the dream is an impossible feat

Thou shalt be over my house, and according to thy words
shall all my people be ruled: only in the throne will I
be greater than thou. And Pharoah said unto Joseph,
See, I have set thee over all of the land of Egypt.

Genesis 41:40, 41

Whatever happens to a dream deferred?

April 12

And when Jesus had cried with a loud voice, he
said Father, into Thy hands I commend my spirit:
and having said thus, he gave up the ghost.

Luke 23:46

Release the need for control
Just let that "thing" go
When you say you've surrendered it all
Demonstrate what you say is really so

And he went a little farther, and fell on his face, and
prayed say, O my Father, if it is possible, let this cup pass
from me: nevertheless not as I will, but as thou wilt.

Matthew 26:39

Truth is indeed demonstration.

April 13

The soul of the sluggard desireth, and hath nothing:
but the soul of the diligent shall be made fat.

Proverbs 13:4

Laziness and slothfulness are interchangeable
Both miss the mark – a sin
Surely we can't expect an extraction
When we've not put anything in

For even when we were with you, this we commanded
you, that if any would not work, neither should he eat.

2 Thessalonians 3:10

Talk is talk; but discipline is doing.

April 14

So when evening was come, the lord of the vineyard saith unto his steward, Call the labourers, and give them their hire, beginning from the last unto the first. And when they came that were hired about the eleventh hour, they received every man a penny.

Matthew 20:8, 9

When you say unjust
I say kind
What you call the fruit
I call the vine

I am the vine, ye are the branches. He that abideth in me, and I in him, the same bringeth forth much fruit; for without me ye can do nothing.

John 15:5

A laborer is worthy of his wages.

He that is slow to anger is better than the mighty; and
he that ruleth his spirit than he that taketh a city.

Proverbs 16:32

Anger is a healthy emotion
That has its place and role
However, it needs assessing often
To ensure adequate and appropriate control

Be ye angry, and sin not: let not the sun go down
upon your wrath. Neither give place to the devil.

Ephesians 4:26, 27

Anger is a **d**ecision before **d**anger.

For the Lord thy God is a consuming fire, even a jealous God.

Deuteronomy 4:24

Take charge, Father God
Our all-consuming fire
Comfort, and correct us
Guide, gird, and inspire

Howbeit when he, the Spirit of truth, is come, he will
guide you into all truth: for he shall not speak of himself;
but whatsoever he shall hear, that shall he speak: and
he will shew you things to come. He shall glorify me:
for he shall receive of mine, and show it to you.

John 16:13, 14

Speak Lord for thy servant hears.

And it came to pass, when Joseph was come unto his brethren, that they stripped Joseph out of his coat, his coat of many colours that was on him. And they took him, and cast him into a pit; and the pit was empty. There was not water in it.

Genesis 37:23, 24

Betrayal is bitter
Whether subtle or blatantly overt
Thank goodness for reconciliation
For a hallelujah after the hurt

And Joseph found grace in his sight, and he served him; and he made him overseer over his house, and all that he had he put into his hand.

Genesis 39:4

Never quit for there's a palace on the other side of the pit.

April 18

And God said unto Moses, I AM THAT I AM;
and he said, Thus shalt thou say unto the children of Israel. I AM hath sent me unto you.

Exodus 3:14

When all is said and done
After a final review of all the peripheral stuff
We'll find out what we should've already known
God's grace is and has always been enough

Jesus said unto them, Verily, verily, I say unto
you, Before Abraham was, I AM.

John 8:58

Whatever it is we think we need or want, He IS.

April 19

Vanities of vanities, saith the Preacher, vanity of
vanities; all is vanity. What profit hath a man of all
of his labour which he taketh under the sun?

Ecclesiastes 1:2, 3

Things and more things
The best that money can buy
Produce emptiness and more emptiness
Because things will placate but never satisfy

Let us hear the conclusion of the whole matter: Fear God, and
keep his commandments: for this is the whole duty of man.

Ecclesiastes 12:13

Practical problems stem from spiritual lack.

April 20

In whom we have redemption through his blood, the forgiveness of sins, according to the riches of his grace; Wherein
he hath abounded toward us in all wisdom and prudence;
Having made known unto us the mystery of his will, according to his good pleasure which he hath purposed in himself.

Ephesians 1:7, 8, 9

A performance orientation hinders Presence
For grace is a gift, not a must
Life sometimes isn't fair
But in God's sovereignty we can trust

Then Job arose, and rent his mantle, and shaved his head, and fell
down upon the ground, and worshipped. And said, Naked came
out of my mother's womb, and naked shall I return thither: The
Lord gave, and the Lord hath taken away, blessed be the name of
the Lord. In all this Job sinned not, nor charged God foolishly.

Job 1:20, 21, 22

Let the redeemed of the Lord say so whom He has redeemed
from the hand of the Enemy.

And God saw every thing that he had made, and behold, it was very good. And the evening and the morning were the sixth day.

Genesis 1:31

When you say secular
I say divine
What you call now
I call, 'in the meantime'

And he said unto me, It is done. I am Alpha and Omega, the beginning and the end. I will give unto him that is athirst of the fountain of the water of life freely. He that overcometh shall inherit all things; I will be his God, and he shall be my son.

Revelation 21:6, 7

Thy kingdom come and Thy perfect will be done.

April 22

Confess your faults one to another, and pray for
another, that ye may be healed. The effectual fervent
prayer of a righteous man availeth much.

James 5:16

The law of confession
Gives Spirit a voice
So what we want to manifest in our lives
Verbally, is a matter of choice

He that covereth his sins shall not prosper: but whosoever confesseth and forsaketh them shall have mercy.

Proverbs 28:13

Speak the Word and let the Word do the work.

April 23

Trust in the Lord with all thine heart; and lean not
unto thine own understanding. In all of thy ways
acknowledge him, and he shall direct thy paths.

Proverbs 3:5, 6

We all have chosen paths
And a Savior that can relate
The promised land is our destination
Although at times we might deviate

I will instruct thee and teach thee in the way which thou shalt
go: I will guide thee with mine eye. Be ye not as the horse, or
as the mule which have no understanding: whose mouth must
be held with bit and bridle, lest they come near unto thee.

Psalm 32:8, 9

Relationship involves repentance. Repentance ensures redemption. Redemption promotes refinement. Refinement promises
restoration. Restoration guarantees reciprocity.

April 24

Give me now wisdom and knowledge, that I may go out and come in before this people: for who can judge this thy people, that is so great? Wisdom and knowledge is granted unto thee; and I will give thee riches, wealth, and honour, such as none of the kings have had that have been before thee, neither shall there any after thee have the like.

2 Chronicles 1:10, 12

Wisdom is the primary building block
There's value in education
Sure, knowledge is power
BUT is useless without activation

And the king said, Bring me a sword. And they brought a sword before the king. And the king said, Divide the living child in two, and give half to the one, and half to the other.

1 Kings 3:24, 25

Knowledge that does not lead to wisdom is useless and of no consequence.

April 25

Then spake Jesus again unto them, saying, I am the
light of the world; he that followeth me shall not
walk in darkness, but shall have the light of life.

John 8:12

Seek light
And follow its lead
Wise men who seek diligently
Find and succeed

And ye shall seek me, and find me, when ye shall search for
me with all your heart. And I will be found by you, saith the
Lord: and I will turn away your captivity, and I will gather you
from all the nations, and from all the places whither I have
driven you, saith the Lord, and I will bring you again into
the place whence I caused you to be carried away captive.

Jeremiah 29:13, 14

Wise men still follow the shining Star.

April 26

For God so loved the world, that he gave his only
begotten Son, that whosoever believeth in him
should not perish, but have everlasting life.

John 3:16

Truly amazing grace
In both beauty and splendor
What can be offered in exchange?
What shall we render?

But God commenedth his love toward us, in that,
while we were yet sinners, Christ died for us.

Romans 5:8

Whosoever will come has redemption without exemption.

For whoever exalteth himself shall be abased; and
he that humbleth himself shall be exalted.

Luke 14:11

Bow down
And completely give in
Humility isn't humiliation
Because in God, every loss is a win

He must increase, but I must decrease.

John 3:30

Whatever, whenever, however, and why-ever.

April 28

For they have healed the hurt of the daughter of my people slightly, saying, Peace, peace where there is no peace.

Jeremiah 8:11

When you say peace
I say confusion
What you call your reality
I call 'just an illusion'

Is there no balm in Gilead; is there no physician there? Why then is not the hearts of the daughter of my people recovered?

Jeremiah 8:22

Judge not according to appearances for appearances are known to be deceptive.

April 29

Seeing it is a righteous thing with God to recompense tribulation to them that trouble you.

2 Thessalonians 1:6

Payback is a given
Restoration heals the pain
Vengeance is His, not ours
And afterwards is the latter rain

The Lord shall open unto thee his good treasure, the heaven to give the rain unto thy land in his season, and to bless all the work of thine hand; and thou shalt lend unto many nations, and thou shalt not borrow. And the Lord shall make thee the head and not the tail; and thou shalt be above only and thou shalt not be beneath; if that thou hearken unto the commandments of the Lord thy God which I command thee this day, to observe and to do them.

Deuteronomy 28:12, 13

The best is yet to come.

April 30

And he said, Unto you it is given to know the mysteries of
the kingdom of God: but to others in parables that seeing
they might not see, and hearing they might not understand.
Now the parable is this: The seed is the word of God.

Luke 8:10, 11

Presently return to the Word
Spend not another moment wallowing in defeat
Remember, remember what to do
Then, repeat and repeat

And when he came to himself, he said, How many hired
servants of my father's have bread enough and to spare, and I
perish with hunger! I will rise and go to my father and will say
unto him, Father, I have sinned against heaven and before thee.

Luke 15:17, 18

Flip the Script and let the Word do the work.

May 1

And not only so, but we glory in tribulations also:
knowing that tribulation worketh patience; and
patience, experience, and experience, hope.

Romans 5:3, 4

There are varied stages of evolution
And our spiritual lot does not make us immune
But only steadfastness in all circumstances
Keeps us watchful and gloriously attuned

Seeing then that we have a great high priest,
that is passed into the heavens, Jesus, the Son
of God, let us hold fast our profession.

Hebrews 4:14

In your patience possess your souls.

May 2

But I say unto you, Love your enemies, bless them that curse you, do good to them that hate you and pray for them which despitefully use you and persecute you.

Matthew 6:44

Yep, it was magnanimously annoying
But try responding in reverse
Being the change you want to see
Means conjuring up the blessing instead of the curse

Our light affliction which is but for a moment, is working for us a far more exceeding and eternal weight of glory.

2 Corinthians 4:17

For His glory is at the end of the story.

And he stretched himself upon the child three times,
and cried unto the Lord, and said, O Lord my God,
I pray thee let this child's soul come into him again.
And the Lord heard the voice of Elijah; and the soul
of the child came into him again, and he revived.

1 Kings 17:21, 22

He did die
BUT yet He arose
Read for yourself
Its not written in prose

But God raised him from the dead.

Acts 13:30

BUT is a small conjunction that serves a tremendous function.

May 4

Verily, verily I say unto you, Except a corn of
wheat fall into the ground and die, it abideth alone;
but if it die, it bringeth forth much fruit.

John 12:24

Sow then harvest
A seed dies in order to grow
But a harvest can't be reaped
When the farmer refuses to sow

The sluggard will not plow by reason of the cold;
therefore shall he beg in harvest and have nothing.

Proverbs 20:4

If you don't sow anything, you certainly won't grow anything.

May 5

Be sober, be vigilant; because your adversary the devil, as a roaring lion, walketh about, seeking whom he may devour.

1 Peter 5:8

The Enemy attacks haters of the status quo
Leaving them scathed and broken
But a sermon best preached is lived out loud
And, some things are better left unspoken

When a man's ways please the Lord, he maketh
even his enemies to be at peace with him.

Proverbs 16:7

Thou preparest a table before me in the presence of my enemies... My cup runneth over.

May 6

In the day of my trouble I sought the Lord: my sore
ran in the night and ceased not: my soul refused to
be comforted. I remembered God and was troubled: I
complained and my spirit was overwhelmed. Selah.

Psalm 77:2, 3

Just when you think the trial is over
Here comes another disturbing letter
Truth is: Trouble often presents itself in 3s
And normally it gets worse before it gets better

I had fainted, unless I had believed to see the goodness of the Lord in the land of the living.

Psalm 27:13

Trials teach us new lessons while tests assess what we've
already learned.

May 7

So likewise, whosoever he be of you that forsaketh
not all that he hath, he cannot be my disciple.

When you say gain
I say loss
Whom you designate servant
I recognize as the boss

But ye shall not be so; but he that is greatest among
you, let him be as the younger; he that is chief, as he
that doth serve. For whether is greater, he that sitteth
at meat, or he that serveth? Is not he that sitteth at
meat? But I am among you as he that serveth.

Luke 22:26, 27

Heavenly help comes via human hearts and human hands.

May 8

The secret of the Lord is with them that fear
him; and he will show them his covenant.

Psalm 25:14

When we lift heart and hands
My Oh My
Mysterious things begin happening
That don't originate from you or I

For the kingdom of God is not in word but in power.

1 Corinthians 4:20

Did not I say to you that if you would believe you would see the
glory of God?

May 9

God is our refuge and strength, a very present help in trouble.

Psalm 46:1

Security is a choice
Acceptance or rejection?
Unlike the guppie in a piranha tank
With God there is protection

He will not suffer thy foot to be moved: he
that keepeth thee will not slumber.

Psalm 121:3

Cling to and clear the air because the Enemy won't play fair.

May 10

For I have satiated the weary soul, and I have
replenished every sorrowful soul.

Jeremiah 31:25

Never, never, never
Though we search far and wide
Will we ever find another
Who's so completely on our side

A man that hath friends must shew himself friendly: and
there is a friend that sticketh closer than a brother.

Proverbs 18:24

When you're down to down to nothing, be assured that God is
up to something.

May 11

Acquaint now thyself with him, and be at peace:
thereby good shall come unto thee.

Job 22:21

Abandon yourself to His will
And stay attuned to His plan
For unless the Lord builds the house
Its structure will never stand

There are many devices in a man heart; nevertheless the counsel of the Lord, that shall stand.

Proverbs 19:21

All is vanity and without Him its all insanity.

May 12

Trust in the Lord with all thine heart; and lean
not unto thine own understanding. In all thy ways
acknowledge him, and he shall direct thy paths.

Proverbs 3:5, 6

The end is a new beginning
There is so much more in store
Transitions are glorious openings
So pray and go confidently through the door

And, behold, I am with thee, and will keep thee in
all places whither thou goest, and will bring thee
again unto this land; for I will not leave thee, until I
have done that which I have spoken to thee of.

Genesis 28:15

When one door closes another one opens.

May 13

It is better to trust in the Lord than to put confidence in man.

Psalm 118:8

Draw your borders
And stand your ground
Both friends and foes will abandon
But only One will stick around

But thou art the same, and thy years shall have no end.

Psalm 102:27

Man will disappoint, disillusion, and dismiss you.

May 14

He that hath knowledge spareth his words: and a
man of understanding is of an excellent spirit.

Proverbs 17:27

What you think is more
I know to be less
What you call failure
I call success

And when he thus had spoken, he cried with
a loud voice, Lazarus, come forth.

John 11:43

Success is failure turned upside down.

May 15

No man can serve two masters: for either he will hate the one, and love the other; or else he will hold to the one, and despise the other. Ye cannot serve God and mammon.

Matthew 6:24

You have a choice
Now rightfully choose
There's only one winning side
And that side won't ever lose

For with God nothing shall be impossible.

Luke 1:37

Choose this day whom ye will serve.

May 16

You will seek and find me when you
seek me with all your heart.

Jeremiah 29:13

It's all or nothing
So let loose the cords
Ties that bind must be unraveled
Better still, they must be destroyed

What, then, shall we say in response to this? If
God is for us, who can be against us?

Romans 8:31

If He is not Lord over it all, He is not Lord at all.

May 17

You are My witnesses says the Lord, and My servant
whom I have chosen that you may know and believe.
And understand that I am He. Before Me there was
no God formed, nor shall there be after Me.

Isaiah 43:10

Satan desires to kill our hopes
Halt progress and get us in a jam
But whatever it is you need on the journey
Remember He is the I AM that I AM

Indeed before the day was, I am He; there is no one who can
deliver out of My hand; I work, and who will reverse it?

Isaiah 43:13

God is the Rock that will never roll.

May 18

We demolish arguments and every pretension that sets
itself up against the knowledge of God, and we take
captive every thought to make it obedient to Christ.

2 Corinthians 10:5

Religiosity is bondage
And can never set us free
Rituals may serve a purpose
But relationship is the magic key

When he had received the drink, Jesus said, It is finished.
With that, he bowed his head and gave up his spirit.

John 19:30

Remember to keep the main thing the main thing.

May 19

Remember this, that the enemy hath reproached,
O Lord, and that the foolish people have blas-
phemed thy name. O let not the oppressed return
ashamed: let the poor and needy praise thy name.

Psalm 74:18, 20

O the circle of life
How the table doth turn
Yesterday I was the student
But today its their time to learn

Wait on the Lord, and keep his way, and he shall exalt thee
to inherit the land: when the wicked are cut off, thou shalt
see it. I have seen the wicked in great power, and spreading himself like a green bay tree. Yet he passed away, and, lo,
he was not: yea, I sought him, but could not be found.

Psalm 37:35, 36, 37

Flipping the Script makes the journey a pleasantly wonderful trip.

May 20

Look to the Lord and his strength: seek his face always.

Psalm 105:4

Be encouraged, my friend
Are you balmy and blue?
Cast your cares on the problem-solver
And watch how He brings you through

Wherefore seeing we also are compassed about, with so
great a cloud of witnesses, let us lay aside every weight, and
the sin which doth so easily beset us, and let us run with
patience the race that is set before us, Looking unto Jesus
the author and finisher of our faith; who for the joy that
was set before him endured the cross, despising the shame,
and is set down at the right hand of the throne of God.

Hebrews 12:1, 2

Ours problems aren't really the problem. The problem is how we
perceive the problem. Now, that's our real problem.

May 21

Blessed is the man that walketh not in the counsel of the
ungodly, nor standeth in the way of sinners, not sitteth in
the seat of the scornful. But his delight is in the law of the
Lord; and in his law doth he meditate day and night.

Psalm 1:1, 2

What you call spending
I call earning
What call teaching
I call learning

I have planted, Apollos watered; but God gave the increase.

1 Corinthians 3:6

Wisdom can only be discerned when we spend time unlearning
the garbage we've already learned.

May 22

Thou wilt keep him in perfect peace, whose mind
is stayed on thee: because he trusteth in thee.

They're not worth it
Trivialities of all different kinds
That birth toxic, disruptive atmospheres
Destructive to the workings of a transforming mind

Finally, brethren, whatsoever things are true, whatsoever
things are honest, whatsoever things are just, whatsoever
things are pure, whatsoever things are lovely, whatsoever things are of good report; if there be any virtue,
and if there be any praise, think on these things.

Philippians 4:8

A mind is a terrible thing to waste.

May 23

And he trembling and astonished said, Lord what wilt thou
have me to do? And the Lord said unto him, Arise, and go
into the city and it shall be told thee what thou must do.

Acts 9:6

An effort in futility
Rebellion is a useless sin
creature versus Creator hasn't a chance
clay against the Potter can't ever win

Humble yourselves therefore under the mighty hand
of God, that he may exalt you in due time.

1 Peter 5:6

Surrender is the highest form of exaltation.

May 24

Neither murmur ye, as some of them also murmured, and were destroyed of the destroyer.

1 Corinthians 10:10

Character trumps comfort
So no need murmuring or complaining
For the Son is always shining
Even when it is raining

And the Lord, he it is that doth go before thee;
he will be with thee, he will not fail thee, neither
forsake thee; fear not, neither be dismayed.

Deuteronomy 31:8

The process is just as important as the product.

2 | Christina Abby

For they being ignorant of God's righteousness, and going about to establish their own righteousness, have not submitted themselves unto the righteousness of God.

Romans 10:3

Sense ain't common to everybody
Exceptional intelligence can make you insane
Stop, see and savor the simple pleasures
There's unparalleled majesty in the meager and mundane

Consider the lilies how they grow; they toil not, they spin not; and yet I say unto you, that Solomon in all his glory was not arrayed like one of these.

Luke 12:27

He who thinks he knows everything doesn't.

May 26

Now the parable is this: The seed is the word of God.

Life has obstacle courses
That must be overcome day by day
Faith is the substance of things hoped for
BUT we must listen, learn, and obey

If you are willing and obedient, you shall eat the good of
the land. But if you refuse and rebel you shall be devoured
by the sword. For the mouth of the Lord hath spoken it.

Isaiah 1:19, 20

Flip the Script and let the Word do the work.

Confess your faults one to another, and pray for
one another that ye may be healed. The effectual
fervent prayer of a righteous man availeth much.

James 5:16

Confront and confess your failures
To family, friend, or foe
You can never be held hostage
When everybody knows what you know

And the peace of God, which passeth all understanding,
shall keep your hearts and mind through Christ Jesus.

Philippians 4:7

Admit to all Truth and deny none.

May 28

But was rebuked for his iniquity: the dumb ass speaking
with a man's voice forbade the madness of the prophet.

2 Peter 2:16

When you say dumb
I say bright
What you call the depth
I call the height

Truth shall spring out of the earth; and righteousness shall look down from heaven.

Psalm 85:11

The farce is on this side of our fulfillment.

May 29

I have said, Ye are gods; and all of you are children of the most High. But you shall die like men, and fall like one of the princes.

Psalm 82:6, 7

Wallowing in defeat?
We're destined to go far
There's Divinity in our nature
So Divine is what we truly are

He lifted me out of a slimy pit, out of the mud and mire; he set my feet on a rock and gave me a firm place to stand. He put a new song in my mouth, a hymn of praise to God.

Psalm 40:2, 3

Our destiny is in our identity and our identity is in our Christ.

May 30

Be not envious against evil men, neither desire to be with them.

Proverbs 24:1

Lying and jealousy
The terrible twins
Parasitic entities by their own right
Who contaminate and destroy our soul from within

These six things doth the Lord hate, yea, seven are an abomination unto him: A proud look, a lying tongue, and hands that shed innocent blood, an heart that deviseth wicked imaginations, feet that be swift in running to mischief, a false witness that speaketh lies, and he that soweth discord among brethren.

Proverbs 6:16, 17, 18, 19

What you don't feed will starve to death.

May 31

So shall my word be that goeth forth out of my mouth; it shall
not return unto me void, but it shall accomplish that which
I please, and it shall prosper in the thing whereto I sent it.

Spiritually, there's no such thing as luck
So no need throwing the dice
The Word precedes designated outcomes
Its reliability is quick and precise

For the word of God is quick, and powerful, and sharper
than any two-edged sword, piercing even to the dividing
asunder of soul and spirit, and of the joints and morrow, and
is a discerner of the thoughts and intents of the heart.

Hebrews 4:12

Speak the Word and let the Word do the work.

June 1

Jesus wept.

Simple can be completely complex
Easily understood but hard to explain
Physical and emotional pain may heal
But deep wounds leave spiritual stains

The sacrifices of God are a broken spirit and a con-
trite heart, O God, thou wilt not despise.

Psalm 51:17

When you change the way you look at things, the very things
you look at change.

June 2

He giveth power to the faint; and to them that
have no might he increaseth strength.

Isaiah 40:29

Life is not over
Feelings won't last
Temporary situations aren't permanent
This too shall pass

For he satisfieth the longing soul, and filleth
the hungry soul with goodness.

Psalm 107:9

The Creator controls both the rising tides and the capsized boats.

June 3

The thief cometh not, but for to steal and to kill,
and to destroy; I am come that they might have life,
and that they might have it more abundantly.

John 10:10

The Enemy's intent is clear
And his cat is out of the bag
His purpose is to destroy us
Not just scare, harass, or nag

Now the Lord is that Spirit; and where the
Spirit of the Lord is, there is liberty.

2 Corinthians 3:17

When the Spirit opens our eyes to see, we can resist the devil
and he will flee.

Enter into his gates with thanksgiving, and into his courts with praise: be thankful unto him, and bless his name.

Psalm 100:4

In trust and thanksgiving
Presence doth we compel
Though our circumstances may remain
All is well, all is well

The Lord reigneth, he is clothed with majesty; the Lord is clothed with strength, wherewith he hath girded himself: the world also is stablished, that it cannot be moved.

Psalm 93:1

God said it so that settles it.

June 5

My heart is inditing a good matter: I speak of
the things which I have made touching the king:
my tongue is the pen of a ready writer.

Psalm 45:1

Testimony can be accomplished
By lifestyle, paper, pencil, pen
We're blessed to be a blessing
To impact another's eternal end

Go ye therefore, and teach all nations, baptizing them
in the name of the Father, and of the Son, and of
the Holy Ghost. Teaching them to observe all things
whatsoever I have commanded you; and, lo, I am
with you always; even unto the end of the world.

Matthew 28:19, 20

Can I get a witness up in here?

Though he slay me, yet will I trust in him: but I will
maintain mine own ways before him. He shall be my
salvation: for an hypocrite shall not come before him.

Job 13:15, 16

Judge not according to appearances
You'll see many contradictions
Illusions aren't reliable sources
So internalizing them is form of spiritual dereliction

Although the fig tree shall not blossom, neither shall fruit
be in the vines; the labour of the olive shall fail; and the
fields shall yield no meat; the flock shall be cut off from
the fold, and there shall be no herd in the stalls. Yet I will
rejoice in the Lord; I will joy in the God of my salvation.

Habakkuk 3:17, 18

The Lord giveth and the Lord taketh away. Blessed be the name
of the Lord.

June 7

But as it is written, Eye hath not seen, nor ear heard,
neither have entered into the heart of man the things
which God hath prepared for them that love them.

1 Corinthians 2:9

> When you say whole
> I say part
> What you call the ear
> I call the heart

And they said one to another, Did not our heart
burn within us while he talked with us by the way,
and while he opened to us the scriptures.

Luke 24:32

Trust and believe in all your heart instead and you'll tame that
old tyrant that's inside your head.

June 8

The Lord shall open unto thee his good treasure, the
heaven to give the rain unto thy land in his season,
and to bless all the work of thine hand: and thou shalt
lend unto many nations and thou shalt not borrow.

Deuteronomy 28:12

Claim the promises
I in the Lord and the Lord in you and me
Whatever happens is already ordained
For everything is predestined to be

Wealth and riches shall be in his house: and
his righteousness endureth forever.

Psalm 112:3

Unclaimed possessions are easily stolen by the Enemy.

June 9

God setteth the solitary in families: he bringeth out those which
are bound with chains; but the rebellious dwell in a dry land.

Psalm 68:6

Tested, tried and true
Listen to the wisdom of the sages
Their insight comes highly recommended
Directly for the indomitable Rock of Ages

Buy the truth and sell it not; also wisdom,
and instruction, and understanding.

Proverbs 23:23

If you want to get to heaven, you have to get through hell first.

June 10

Be strong and of a good courage, fear not, nor be afraid
of them: for the Lord thy God, he it is that doth go
with thee; he will not fail thee, nor forsake thee.

Deuteronomy 31:6

The Enemy of our soul
Would have us trembling in fear
To blind our vision of Love
And forget that He's ever-presently near

God is our refuge and strength, a very
present help in time of trouble.

Psalm 46:1

Rock of Ages, let me hide myself in Thee.

June 11

And I John saw the holy city, new Jerusalem, coming down
from God out of heaven, prepared as a bride adorned
for her husband. And I heard a great voice out of heaven
saying, Behold, the tabernacle of God is with men, and
he will dwell with them, and they shall be his people, and
God himself shall be with them, and be their God.

Revelation 21:1, 2, 3

Pray. Penetrate the darkness
See the other side of eternity
Catch the royal vision
And bask in its mesmerizing clarity

And immediately there fell from his eyes as it had been scales;
and he received sight forthwith, and arose, and was baptized.

Acts 9:18

Prayer is the bridge between panic and peace.

June 12

The righteous shall flourish like the palm tree:
he shall grow like a cedar in Lebanon.

Psalm 92:12

Like the resiliency of a palm
That relies upon its internal sap
Storms only strengthen our roots
And reveal ours and others handicaps

Those that be planted in the house of the Lord
shall flourish in the courts of our God.

Psalm 92:13

Without adequate sap, we're all apt to snap.

June 13

The law of the Lord is perfect, converting the soul; the testimony of the Lord is sure, making wise the simple.

Psalm 19:7

The beacon of hope
Prevents man's perpetual see-saw
But what kind of kingdom could properly function
Without statutes, rules or law

I have longed for thy salvation, O Lord;
and thy law is my delight.

A Bible that's falling apart reveals a saint who ain't.

June 14

And he said, This will I do: I will pull down my barns, and build
greater; and there will I bestow all my fruits and my goods.
And I will say to my soul, Soul, thou hast much goods laid
up for many years; take thine ease, eat, drink, and be merry.

Luke 12:18, 19

When you say comfort
I say need
What you call benevolence
I call pride and greed

But when thou doest alms, let not thy left hand know what
they right hand doeth. That thine alms may be in secret; and thy
Father which seeth in secret himself shall reward thee openly.

Matthew 6:3, 4

When you do what you do without expectation, you'll never
be disappointed.

June 15

And he began to say unto them, This day is
this scripture fulfilled in your ears.

Luke 4:21

Eventually, but certainly
Trust that we're almost there
Love will be birthed in its surest, purest form
No more terror, torment, despair

And God shall wipe away all tears from their eyes; and there
shall be no more death, neither sorrow, nor crying, neither shall
there be any more pain; for the former things are passed away.

Revelation 21:4

Trust doesn't require understanding but just a little bit of faith.

June 16

For who hath known the mind of the Lord, that he
may instruct him? But we have the mind of Christ.

1 Corinthians 2:16

Omniscient in power and province
Misinterpreted and often misunderstood
But his Word comes with a guarantee
That's always intended for our highest good

For I know the thoughts that I think toward you, saith the Lord,
thoughts of peace, and not of evil, to you an expected end.

Jeremiah 29:11

Flip the Script and let the Word do the work.

June 17

For godly sorrow worketh repentance to salvation not to be repented of: but the sorrow of the world worketh death.

2 Corinthians 7:10

This season is marred in tears
The most bitter you've ever tasted
Be encouraged, stay focused and faithful
For nothing, nothing is ever wasted

And we know that all things work together for good to them that love God, to them who are called according to his purpose.

Romans 8:28

They that sow in tears shall reap in joy.

June 18

Now there are diversities of gifts, but the same Spirit.

Spiritual gifts are for the furtherance of the kingdom
So let not their purpose be misunderstood
Self-aggrandizement leads to a dead end
BUT dividends are compounded when
focused on the common good

But the fruit of the Spirit is love, joy, peace, long-suffering, gentleness, goodness, faith, meekness, temperance; against such there is no law.

Galatians 5:22, 23

Relate then operate.

June 19

The wind bloweth where it listeth, and thou hearest the sound thereof, but canst not tell whence it cometh, and whither it goeth; so is every one that is born of the Spirit.

John 3:8

Regardless of our current standing
We're still a spiritual being
So enjoy this privileged position
After the winter comes the blossoming spring

I have seen the wicked in great power, and spreading himself like a green bay tree. Yet he passed away, and, lo, he was not: yea, I sought him, but he could not be found.

Psalm 37:35, 36

We are spiritual beings going through a human experience not human beings going through a spiritual experience.

June 20

Bless the Lord, O my soul: and all that is
within me, bless his holy name.

Know that praise summons Presence
While ingratitude drives Him away
This revelation will come later
Though you might be confused today

They reel to and fro, and stagger like a drunken man, are
at their wit's end. Then they cry unto the Lord in their
trouble, and he bringeth them out of their distresses.

Psalm 107:27, 28

Knowing isn't a function of the head but a function of the heart.

June 21

But seek ye first the kingdom of God, and his righteousness; and all these things shall be added unto you.

Matthew 6:33

When you say last
I say first
What you call hunger
I call thirst

As the hart panteth after the water brooks, so
panteth my soul after thee, O God.

Psalm 42:1

Put first things first.

June 22

And he said, Who told thee that thou wast naked?
Hast thou eaten of the tree, whereof I commanded thee that thou shouldest not eat?

Genesis 3:11

Our normal is abnormal
An absolute anomaly
How can a manacled mind
Ever be interpreted as being free?

They answered him, We be Abraham's seed, and were never in
bondage to any man; how sayest thou, Ye shall be made free?

John 8:33

An open mind has a room with a view and a soften heart makes
all things anew.

June 23

I and my Father are one.

There is a new normal
When all is said and done
There's also universality in individuality
And power in being in One

That they should seek the Lord, if haply they might feel after
him, and find him, though he be not far from every one of us.
For in him we live, and move, and have our being; as certain
also of your own poets have said, For we are also his offspring.

Acts 17:27, 28

Oneness with the Source is oneness with all manifestation.

And let us not be weary in well doing for in
due season, we shall reap, if we faint not.

Galatians 6:9

Run the race before you
Though things may look bleak
We weren't designed to look into the future
Where there's a valley, there's also a peak

Jesus said unto him, If thou canst believe, all
things are possible to him that believeth.

Mark 9:23

The promised land is on the other side of the wilderness.

June 25

One thing have I desired of the Lord, that will I seek after; that I may dwell in the house of the Lord all of the days of my life, to behold the beauty of the Lord, and to enquire in his temple.

Psalm 27:4

It ain't over yet
All is well
The battle isn't yours
So believe, trust and dwell

Surely goodness and mercy shall follow me all the days of my life: and I will dwell in the house of the Lord forever.

Psalm 23:6

When you begin to doubt God know that the Enemy is doing his job.

June 26

And I will restore to you the years that the locust hath eaten, the cankerworm, and the caterpillar, and the palmerworm, my great army which I sent among you.

Joel 2:25

Enter the place called Dwell
Nothing there is dead
What has been cut off is really being cut in
So keep your mind on restoration instead

So the Lord blessed the latter end of Job more than his beginning: for he had fourteen thousand sheep, and six thousand camels, and a thousand yoke of oxen, and a thousand she asses.

Job 42:12

As we spiritually mature so does our desire and capacity to endure.

June 27

For I know nothing by myself, yet am I not hereby
justified: but he that judgeth me is the Lord.

1 Corinthians 4:4

The world doesn't revolve
Around what we believe and think we know
Until narcissism is eradicated
Global healing has a long way to go

For grace are ye saved through faith, and that
not of yourselves; it is the gift of God.

Ephesians 2:8

Mortify ourselves then magnify Him.

June 28

Love worketh no ill to his neighbor: therefore love is the fulfilling of the law.

When you say hatred
I say love
When you say below
I say above

Set your affection on things above, not on things on the earth.

Colossians 3:2

Love is the overpass that connects us to the highway to heaven.

June 29

Who is this that darkeneth counsel by
words without knowledge?

Job 38:2

He can't be adequately described
He's is more than just great
Much holier, wiser, bigger, and better
Than our vocabulary could ever define or create

For who hath known the mind of the Lord? Or who hath been
his counselor? Or who hath first given to him, and it shall be
recompensed unto him again. For of him, and through him,
and to him, are all things: to whom be glory forever. Amen.

Romans 11:34, 35, 36

His sovereignty is superior and His essence is unimagin-
ably indescribable.

Yea, the darkness hideth not from thee; but the night shineth
as the day: the darkness and the light are both alike to thee.

Psalm 139:7

Possibilities are in problems
Raw nuggets of pure gold
So look for them while going through
Sacred secrets He'll unfold

Arise, shine for thy light is come, and the
glory of the Lord is risen upon thee.

Isaiah 60:1

Within the problem lies its own solution.

July 1

A slothful man hideth his hand in his bosom, and
will not so much as bring it to his mouth again.

Proverbs 19:24

Stuck on stupid?
Own your shame
Projection is unreasonably unproductive
For no one else is to blame

Love not sleep, lest thou come to poverty; open thine
eyes, and thou shalt be satisfied with bread.

Proverbs 20:13

Expect the terror and torment to stay when we choose to cling
to our old way.

July 2

Every branch in me that beareth not fruit he
taketh away; and every branch that beareth fruit, he
purgeth it, that it may bring forth more fruit.

John 15:2

Pruning is essential to growth
Shears are the tool of attack
Removal of old makes room for the new
Exponentially, what's lost comes back

They shall still bring forth fruit in old age;
they shall be fat and flourishing.

Psalm 92:14

The hurtful sting dissipates when we add insight to our injuries.

July 3

That no flesh should glory in his presence. That, according
as it is written, He that glorieth, let him glory in the Lord.

1 Corinthians 1:29, 31

His Spirit and His glory alone
Should be our heart's desire
But our fleshly tendencies can only be remedied
By our going through the fire

Take away the dross from the silver, and there
shall come forth a vessel for the finer.

Proverbs 25:4

Iron sharpens iron.

July 4

But made himself no reputation, and took upon him
the form of a servant, and was made in the likeness of
men. And being found in fashion as a man he humbled
himself, and became obedient unto death, even the death
of the cross. Wherefore God also hath highly exalted him,
and given him a name which is above every name.

Philippians 2:7, 8, 9

Sometimes the benefits acquired
Far outweigh any loss
Though our role might appear subordinate
Servanthood trumps being boss

I beseech you therefore brethren, by the mercies of God,
that ye present your bodies a living sacrifice, holy, acceptable unto God, which is your reasonable service.

Romans 12:1

Try not dismissing the notion that subordination may actually be
a promotion.   .

July 5

And be not conformed to this world; but be ye transformed
by the renewing of your mind, that ye may prove what
is that good, and acceptable, and perfect, will of God.

Romans 12:2

Challenge mass consciousness
The orthodoxy of status quo
Conventional wisdom isn't the proven panacea
So decide now what way you wish to go

Behold, I will do a new thing; not it shall spring
forth; shall ye not know it? I will even make a way
in the wilderness, and rivers in the desert.

Isaiah 43:19

Those who continue to swallow the lies of the Enemy will
invariably choke on them.

July 6

And the Lord shall make thee the head, and not the tail; and thou shalt be above only, and thou shalt not be beneath; if that thou hearken unto the commandments of the Lord thy God, which I command thee this day, to observe and to do them.

Deuteronomy 28:13

Try assessing the situation differently
Obviously, you can be trusted with trouble
Your faith is being tested
And your recompense will be double

If a man shall deliver unto his neighbor money or stuff to keep, and it be stolen out of the man's house; if the thief be found, let him pay double.

Exodus 22:7

When the student is ready the Teacher will show up.

July 7

He answered and said unto them, Well hath Esaias prophesied
of you hypocrites, as it is written, This people honoureth
me with their lips, but their heart is far from me.

Mark 6:6

When you say sacred
I say profane
What you call extreme fundamentalism
I call preposterously insane

For I desired mercy, and not sacrifice and the knowledge of God more than burnt offerings.

Hosea 6:6

Hypocrites are people who are not themselves on Sundays.

This book of the law shall not depart out of thy mouth;
but thou shalt meditate therein day and night, that thou
mayest observe to do according to all that is written
therein: for then thou shalt make thy way prosperous, and then thou shall have good success.

Joshua 1:8

Ponder and meditate
Strategize and assess
Think clearly before proceeding
The land is still yours to possess

That in blessing I will bless thee, and in multiply-
ing I will multiply thy seed as the stars of heaven,
and as the sand which is upon the sea shore; and
thy seed shall possess the gate of his enemies.

Genesis 22:17

Flip the Script and let the Word do the work.

July 9

For we walk by faith, not by sight.

2 Corinthians 5:7

It matters not what we see or hear
Nor what we tend to feel
Our intangibles are our true treasures
For the invisible is far more real

Now thanks be unto God, which always causeth
us to triumph in Christ, and maketh manifest the
savour of his knowledge by us in every place.

2 Corinthians 2:14

The Invisible is more real than anything you or I may ever see.

July 10

He that refuseth instruction despiseth his own soul;
but he that heareth reproof getteth understanding.

Proverbs 15:32

To believe or not believe
Is a matter of consequence and choice
But the more we walk, look and listen
The more we'll hear and know His voice

And when he putteth forth his own sheep, he goeth
before them, and the sheep follow him; for they know
his voice. And a stranger will they not follow, but will flee
from him: for they know not the voice of strangers.

John 10:4, 5

Life teaches us wonderful lessons if we would but stop, think,
look, and listen.

July 11

And not many days after the younger son gathered all together, and took his journey into a far country and there he wasted his substance with riotous living. And when he has spent all, there arose a mighty famine in the land, and he began to be in want.

Luke 15:13, 14

The journey of life
Has many pit stops and stations
But like the prodigal's change in mind
We're allowed to return from our nightmarish vacations

And when he came to himself, he said, How many hired servants of my father's have bread enough and to spare, and I perish with hunger! I will arise and go to my father, and will say unto him, Father, I have sinned against heaven, and before thee.

Luke 15:17, 18

Something that can't continue won't.

July 12

A gift is as a precious stone in the eyes of him that
hath it; whithersoever it turneth, it prospereth.

Proverbs 17:8

Hardship and heartaches
Are our least favored gifts
But they're invaluable in spurning growth
Because they shake, break and sift

Therefore I take pleasure in infirmities, in reproaches,
in necessities, in persecutions, in distresses for Christ's
sake: for when I am weak, then I am strong.

2 Corinthians 12:10

The comfort zone is the place to be, we think; but in the bigger
scheme of things, our stagnation actually stinks.

July 13

He that getteth wisdom loveth his own soul: he
that keepeth understanding shall find good.

Proverbs 19:8

No investment, no return
So get up and take action
The Enemy is a liar
So don't give him no satisfaction

And the God of peace shall bruise Satan under your feet
shortly. The grace of our Lord Jesus Christ be with you.

Romans 16:20

God is our vindicator so our haters should be our greatest
motivators.

And the serpent said unto the woman, ye shall not surely die. For God doth know that in the day ye eat thereof, then your eyes shall be opened, and ye shall be as gods, knowing good and evil.

Genesis 3:4, 5

What you call truth
I call the big fat lie
What you call unmitigated deceit
I call the modus operandi

Be sober, be vigilant; because your adversary the devil, as a roaring lion, walketh about seeking whom he may devour.

1 Peter 5:8

We've been had. We've been hoodwinked. We have been bamboozled.

July 15

For the love of money is the root of all evil; which while
some coveted after, they have erred from the faith, and
pierced themselves through with many sorrows.

1Timothy 6:10

Money is a medium of exchange
That can procure power and clout
It can never buy peace of mind
BUT it takes a while for us to figure that out

There is an evil which I have seen under the sun, and
it is common among men; A man to whom God hath
given riches, wealth, and honour, so that he wanteth
nothing for his soul of all that he desireth, yet God
giveth him not power to eat thereof, but a stranger
eateth it; this is vanity, and it is an evil disease.

Ecclesiastes 6:1, 2

I'd rather have peace of mind than a piece of money.

July 16

I am Alpha and Omega, the beginning and the
ending, saith the Lord, which is, and which was,
and which is to come, the Almighty.

Revelation 1:8

Nothing is impossible with God
Everything has purpose and reason
BUT His sovereignty of the universe
Dictates His timing in His due season

And he shall be like a tree planted by the rivers of water,
that bringeth forth his fruit in his season; his leaf also shall
not wither; and whatsoever he doeth shall prosper.

Psalm 1:3

You can't hurry Love; you just have to wait.

For thus saith the Lord unto the house of
Israel, Seek ye me, and ye shall live.

Amos 5:4

Time is spent
Gray hairs have begun to grow
A harvest is unrealistic
When one refuses to sow

For I have no pleasure in the death of him that dieth, saith
the Lord God; wherefore turn yourselves, and live ye.

Ezekiel 18:32

Unless a grain of wheat falls to the ground and dies, it
remains alone.

July 18

To appoint unto them that mourn in Zion, to give
unto them beauty for ashes, the oil of joy for mourn-
ing, the garment of praise for the spirit of heaviness,
that they might be called trees of righteousness, the
planting of the Lord, that he might be glorified.

Isaiah 61:3

Cease struggling and striving
Know and clearly gauge your domain
And respect the limit of your capacity
For control will lead to needless pain

And all this assembly shall know that the Lord
saveth not with sword and spear: for the battle is the
Lord's, and he will give you into our hands.

1 Samuel 17:47

Stand still and see the salvation of the Lord.

July 19

For which cause I also suffer these things; nevertheless I am not ashamed: for I know whom I have believed,
and am persuaded that he is able to keep that which
I have committed unto him against that day.

2Timothy 1:12

Beaten, bruised, battered
Can't take it any more
Remember, inside the seed is your potential
So your best yet is in store

For I reckon the sufferings of this present time are not worthy
to be compared with the glory which shall be revealed in us.

Romans 8:18

From glory to glory to glory.

July 20

Thou feedest them with the bread of tears; and
givest them tears to drink in great measure.

Psalm 80:5

No eternal gain without pain
A Truth we'd like to avoid or buffer
But if we plan to reign with Christ
We must also be willing to suffer

And if children, then heirs; heirs of God, and joint-
heirs with Christ; if so be that we suffer with
him, that we may also be glorified together.

Romans 8:17

Through preparation and perseverance we obtain the promises.

July 21

But as for you, ye thought evil against me; but
God meant it unto good, to bring to pass as it
is this day, to save much people alive.

Genesis 50:20

When you say evil
I say good
What you call mystical
I call misunderstood

And the light shineth in darkness; and the
darkness comprehended it not.

John 1:5

All things work together for the good of those who love the
Lord and are called according to his purpose.

July 22

They are corrupt, and speak wickedly concerning oppression; they speak loftily. For all day long I
have plagued and chastened every morning.

Psalm 73:8, 14

While the battle rages on
The Enemy will taunt and brag
But the outcome has already been fixed
No need to wag a white flag

When I thought to know this, it was too painful for me: Until
I went into the sanctuary of God; then understood I their end.

Psalm 73:16, 17

He who laughs last laughs the longest.

July 23

But godliness with contentment is great gain.

Don't give the Enemy ammunition
Stop complaining about what God hasn't done for you
Start praising Him for what He has done
And just wait for your next breakthrough

Let your conversation be without covetousness and
be content with such things as ye have; for he hath
said, I will never leave thee, nor forsake thee.

Hebrews 13:5

Refuse and confuse the accuser.

July 24

For the kingdom of heaven is as a man travel-
ling into a far country, who called his own servants, and delivered unto them his goods.

Matthew 25:14

Talent might open doors
But discipline is the keeper of progress
Arrogance is a surefire altitude deflator
While attitude determines success

His lord said unto him, Well done, thou good and faithful
servant; thou has been faithful over a few things, I will make
thee ruler over many things: enter thou into the joy of they lord.

Matthew 25:21

Our attitude determines our altitude.

July 25

If any of you lack wisdom, let him ask of God, that giveth to all men liberally, and unbraideth not; and it shall be given him.

James 1:5

Knowledge is crucial
Yet cannot compare to what wisdom brings
It can expand the intellectual repertoire
But wisdom is the prime and principal thing

When wisdom entered into the heart, and knowledge is pleasant unto thy soul; discretion shall preserve thee, understanding shall keep thee: to deliver thee from the way of the evil man, from the man that speaketh forward things.

Proverbs 2:10, 11, 12

Knowledge is the understanding that helps you make the peanut butter and bread. Wisdom is the instrument that helps you apply the spread.

July 26

And no marvel; for Satan himself is transformed into an angel of light.

Search the scriptures
And you'll finally deduce
Satan is an impotent imposter
That tries to emulate but can't reproduce

Search the scriptures, for in them ye think ye have
eternal life: and they are they which testify of me.

John 5:39

The Enemy may imitate but can never replace nor replicate
his Creator.

Flippin The Script 1207

Let the lying lips be put to silence; which speak grievous
things proudly and contemptuously against the righteous.

Psalm 31:18

You may now be a victim
Much to your dismay
But there's a lesson to be learned by the perpetrator also
So respond to the situation in an uncommon way

When the Lord turned again the captivity of Zion, we were
like them that dream. There was our mouth filled with
laughter, and our tongue with singing; then said they among
the heathen, the Lord hath done great things for them.

Psalm 126:1, 2

It's the right time and right place for both victim and perpetrator to grow in grace.

July 28

But new wine must be put in new
bottles, and both are preserved.

Luke 5:38

When you say old
I say new
What you call yellow
I call blue

But he himself went a day's journey into the wilderness, and
came and sat down under a juniper tree: and he requested
for himself that he might die, and said, It is enough; now, O
Lord, take away my life, for I am not better than my fathers.

1 Kings 19:4

Recall and rely upon His strength and might when you're dis-
couraged and too weak to fight.

July 29

Whither shall I go from thy spirit? Or whither shall I flee
from thy presence? If I ascend up into heaven, thou art
there: if I make my bed in hell, behold, thou art there.

Psalm 139:7, 8

Bitter are your current tears
Like none you've ever tasted
Weeping may last for a time
But, remember, nothing is ever wasted

The Lord will perfect that which concer-
neth me; thy mercy, O Lord, endureth forever:
forsake not the works of thine own hand.

Psalm 138:8

Like the finger and its nail, He knows our shortcomings
very well.

I returned, and saw under the sun, that the race is not to the swift, nor the battle to the strong, neither yet bread to the wise, nor yet riches to me of understanding, nor yet favour to men of skill; but time and chance happeneth to them all.

Ecclesiastes 9:11

He can empathize with your frustration
But nobody can run your race
Soldiers prepare for their battles
And the best get to go to the worst place

But the Lord said unto him, Go thy way: for he is a chosen vessel unto me, to bear my name before the Gentiles, and kings, and the children of Israel. For I will shew him how great things he must suffer for my name's sake.

Acts 9:15, 16

Smooth seas rarely make good sailors.

July 31

Come now, and let us reason together saith the
Lord, though your sins be as scarlet, they shall be
as white as snow; though they be as wool.

Isaiah 1:18

Nothing is achieved in a vacuum
Success takes concentrated cooperation
Single-mindedness in purpose
Will foster unheard of multiplication

And these are they which are sown on good ground; such
as hear the word, and receive it, and bring forth fruit,
some thirtyfold, some sixty, and some an hundred.

Mark 5:20

Our strength is in our struggle.

August 1

How are thou fallen from heaven, O Lucifer, son of
the morning! How are thou cut down to the ground,
which didst weaken the nations! For thou hast said in
thine heart, I will ascend into heaven, I will exalt my
throne above the stars of God; I will sit also upon the
mount of the congregation, in the sides of the north.

Isaiah14:12, 13

The Enemy has a mission
Without shame or compunction
Accusing and opposing is his job
And there's no need begrudging his function

And I heard a loud voice saying in heaven, Now is come
salvation, and strength, and the kingdom of our God, and the
power of his Christ; for the accuser of our brethren is cast
down, which accused them before our God day and night.

Revelation 12:10

The whole world is a stage and everybody plays a part.

August 2

It shall come to pass in that day: That his burden will be taken away from your shoulder, and his yoke from your neck, and the yoke will be destroyed because of the anointing.

Isaiah 10:27

Nothing is too hard
His presence is not meant to scare
Nor does His love torment
And, yes, yes He really does care

Come unto me, all ye that labour and are heavy lade, and I will give you rest. Take my yoke upon you, and learn of me; for I am meek and lowly in heart: and ye shall find rest unto your souls. For my yoke is easy, and my burden is light.

Matthew 11:28, 29, 30

Cast all of your fears and burdens upon Him for He cares for you.

August 3

Be sober, be vigilant; because your adversary the devil; as a roaring lion walketh about seeking whom he may devour.

1 Peter 5:8

If but a moment in time
He'll continue hanging around
But like the mythical Icarus
The Enemy is gonna go down!

Therefore rejoice, ye heavens, and ye that dwell in them. Woe to the inhibiters of the earth and of the sea! For the devil is come down unto you, having great wrath, because he knoweth that he hath but a short time.

Revelation 12:12

Empty wagons rattle the loudest.

August 4

The way of a fool is right in his own eyes; but
he that hearkeneth unto counsel is wise.

A manipulated mind
Concedes wrong for right
But Truth-bearers hold on to Truth for Truth sake
And are prepared for a spirited fight

Fight the good fight of faith, lay hold of eternal
life, whereunto thou are also called, and hast pro-
fessed a good profession before many witnesses.

1Timothy 6:12

The battle is waged in our minds.

226 | Christina Abbu

August 5

They eyes of the Lord are in every place,
beholding the evil and the good.

Proverbs 15:3

See, but don't react
Everything doesn't require our attention
Distractions can be deceitfully deadly
Ignore and beat the Enemy at his own inventions

He that handleth a matter wisely shall find good:
and whoso trusteth in the Lord, happy is he.

Proverbs 16:20

Open your mind before the Enemy opens your mouth.

August 6

Yet a little sleep, a little slumber, a little folding of
the hands to sleep; so shall thy poverty come as one
that travelleth, and thy want as an armed man.

Proverbs 6:10, 11

Indecisiveness and procrastination
Invariably makes waste
But when opportunity knocks
Its time to make haste

And when Jesus came to the place, he looked up, and
saw him, and said unto him, Zacchaeus, make haste, and
come down; for today I must abide at thy house. And he
made haste, and came down, and received him joyfully.

Luke 19:5, 6

When opportunity knocks, it demands an immediate answer.

August 7

And the devil, taking him up into an high mountain, shewed unto him all the kingdoms of the world in a moment in time.

Luke 4:4

When you say permanent
I say temporary
What you call double-mindedness
I call the perpetual adversary

If any of you lack wisdom, let him ask of God, that giveth to all men liberally, and upbraideth not; and it shall be given to him. But let him ask in faith, nothing wavering. For he that wavereth is like a wave of the sea driven with the wind and tossed. For let not that man think that he shall receive any thing of the Lord. A double-minded man is unstable in all his ways.

James 1:5, 6, 7, 8

You believe that there is one God, you do well.

August 8

Then Jesus turned, and saw them following, and saith unto them, What seek ye? They said unto him, Rabbi (which is to say, being interpreted, Master,) where dwellest thou?

John 1:38

Spectators and participators
Are not one in the same
Watching isn't doing
You've got to have skin in the game

He saith unto them, Come and see. They came
and saw where he dwelt, and abode with him
that day; for it was about the tenth hour.

John 1:39

Its not going to the work unless you work it!

August 9

He that believeth on me, as the scripture hath said,
out of his belly will flow rivers of living water.

John 6:38

Independence will leave you lonely
While interdependence helps ward off despair
Self-sufficiency propagates spiritual sorrow
Our willingness to collaborate is a serious affair

For David is not ascended into the heaven: but he
saith himself, the Lord said unto my Lord, sit thou on
my right hand until I make thy foes thy footstool.

Acts 2:34, 35

God is connected to man like the finger is to the hand.

August 10

For what saith the scripture? Abraham believed God,
and it was counted unto him for righteousness.

Romans 4:3

Our sins have been forgiven
So we're no longer sinners
When our mind wraps around that reality
We'll begin thinking and acting like winners

Saying, Blessed are those whose iniquities are forgiven, and whose sins are covered. Blessed is the
man to whom the Lord will not impute sin.

Romans 4:7, 8

Flip the Script and let the Word do the work.

August 11

Why are thou cast down, O my soul? And why art thou disquieted with me? Hope in God; for I shall yet praise him who is the health of my countenance and my God.

Psalm 43:5

On the brink of brokenness
Barely hanging on by a thread
Done lost everything and everybody
But I refuse to lose my head

All this is come upon us; yet have we not forgotten thee, neither have we dealt falsely in thy covenant.

Psalm 44:17

Regardless of our circumstances, the safest place to be is in the will of God.

August 12

Now it came to pass on a certain day; that he went into a
ship with his disciples; and he said unto them, Let us go over
unto the other side of the lake. And they launched forth.

Movement sometimes translates misery
Chaos and inconsistency with the norm
But when its time, its time for transition
So be prepared for your desert storm

Bust as they sailed he fell asleep: and there came down
a storm of wind on the lake; and they were filled
with water, and were in jeopardy. And they came to
him, and awoke him, saying Master, master, we perish.
The he arose, and rebuked the wind and the raging of
the water; and they ceased, and there was a calm.

Luke 8:23, 24

A new level always summons a new devil.

August 13

Put on the whole armour of God that ye may be
able to stand against the wiles of the devil.

Ephesians 6:11

So you've made the commitment
Know that hell is about to break loose
Without true grit and unwavering faith
The Enemy is bent on cooking your goose

Cast not away therefore your confidence which hath great
recompence of reward. For ye have need of patience, that after
you have done the will of God ye might receive the promise.

Hebrews 10:35, 36

By faith they passed through the Red Sea as if on dry land.

August 14

They answered him, We be Abraham's seed, and were never in
bondage to any man: how sayest thou, Ye shall be made free?

John 8:33

When you say loose
I say bound
What you call square
I call round

Be not deceived, God is not mocked: for whatsoever a man soweth, that shall he also reap.

Galatians 6:7

It ain't no secret what God can do.

August 15

But the transgressors shall be destroyed together:
the end of the wicked shall be cut off.

Things alter rapidly
And can flip in a snap
So sit back and watch in patience
While the evildoers trip in their own trap

And Esther said, The adversary and enemy is this wicked
Ha-man. Then Ha-man was afraid before the king and
queen. So they hanged Ha-man on the gallows that he had
prepared for Mordecai. Then was the king's wrath pacified.

Esther 7:6, 10

He who digs a ditch better dig two; for the one dug for somebody else will be the one he falls into.

August 16

Forever O Lord your word is settled in heaven.

I got inside that door
Because I believed I could
It flung wide open for me
God said it would

For with God nothing shall be impossible.

Luke 1:37

Prayer is the key while faith unlocks the door.

238 | Christina Abby

Thy pomp is brought down to the grave, and the noise
of thy viols: the worm is spread under thee, and the
worms cover thee. How art thou fallen from heaven, O
Lucifer, son of the morning! How art thou cut down
to the ground, which didst weaken the nations.

Isaiah 14:11, 12

He spoke the universe into existence
What a mighty God we serve
To think the creature could best its Creator
Huh, only Satan would have the nerve

But if it be of God ye cannot overthrown it; let
haply ye be found even to fight against God.

Acts 5:39

Our arms are too short to box with God.

August 18

Surely your turning things upside down shall be esteemed
as the potter's clay: for shall the work say of him that
made it, He made me not? Or shall the thing framed
say of him that framed it, He had no understanding?

Isaiah 29:16

Oh the depth of riches of His wisdom
Only the surface can we barely scratch
The brightest of our brightest can't compete
No, not one, can or will ever match

And thou Lord, in the beginning hast laid the foundation of the
earth; and the heavens are the works of thine hands. They shall
perish; but thou remainest; and they all shall wax old as doth a
garment; And as a vesture shalt thou fold them up, and they shall
be changed; but Thou art the same, and thy years shall not fail.

Hebrews 1:10, 11, 12

His depth defines our dimension and His dimension determines
our destiny.

And he that sat upon the throne said, Behold, I make all things new. And he said unto me; Write: for these words are true and faithful. And he said unto them, It is done. I am Alpha and Omega, the beginning and the end. I will give unto him that is athirst of the fountain of the water of life freely.

Revelation 21:5, 6

Everything is presently settled
In preparation for the head on collision
Light has already overtaken the darkness
And this Truth is not open for revision

And there shall be no night there; and they need no candle, neither light of the sun; for the Lord God giveth them light; and they shall reign for ever and ever.

Revelation 22:5

Begin again with this end in mind.

August 20

Is there no balm in Gilead? Is there no physician there? Why then is not the health of the daughter of my people recovered?

Jeremiah 8:22

Wipe away your tears
Put on a big smile
The weight of the scales is shifting
Hold on for just a little while

Though I walk in the midst of trouble, thou wilt revive me: thou shalt stretch forth thine hand against the wrath of mine enemies, and thy right hand shall save me.

Psalm 138:7

Our purpose will sustain us through whatever it is that pains us.

August 21

O death where is thy sting? O grave where is thy victory?

When you say tragedy
I say triumph
What you call an abyss
I call a bump

The Lord upholdeth all that fall, and raiseth
up all those that be bowed down.

Psalm 145:14

God always has a ram in the bush.

August 22

Is any among you afflicted? Let him pray.
Is any merry? Let him sing praises.

Take that nagging problem to the altar
Leave it there in capable hands
Logically, you might not ever rationalize it
So don't frustrate yourself trying to understand

The Lord will give strength unto his people;
the Lord will bless his people with peace.

Psalm 29:11

Let Go and Let God.

As unknown, and yet well known; as dying, and, behold, we live, as chastened, and not killed. As sorrowful, yet always rejoicing; as poor, yet making many rich; as having nothing, and yet possessing all things.

2 Corinthians 6:9, 10

Want out of the funk?
This might sound odd
But when the aroma becomes putrid
Just start praising God

And we are his witnesses of these things; and so is also the Holy Ghost, who God hath given them that obey him.

Acts 5:32

When we become reflective, there's a complete change in our perspective.

August 24

God is not a man, that he should lie; neither the son of man, that he should repent: hath he said, and shall he not do it? Or hath he spoken, and shall not he make it good?

Numbers 23:19

Action is observable substance
And our words destroy or invigorate
If our actions and words don't edify
We can't expect God to cooperate

He hath shewed thee, O man, what is good: and what doth the Lord require of thee, but to do justly and love mercy, and to walk humbly with thy God.

Micah 6:8

If you can't say something good about someone, just say nothing.

August 25

For I was envious of the foolish, when I saw the prosperity of the wicked. They are not in trouble as other
men neither are they plagued like other men.

Psalm 73:3, 5

It's all about strategy
And your opponent will make a mistake
The game will then turn in your favor
OOPS! Checkmate

Thus saith the Lord the King of Israel, and his
redeemer the Lord of hosts; I am the first, and I
am the last; and beside me there is no God.

Isaiah 44:6

Every dog has its day and a dirty one has two.

And Jacob was left alone; and there wrestled a man
with him until the breaking of the day. And he
said, Let me go, for the day breaketh. And he said,
I will not let thee go, except thou bless me.

Genesis 32:24, 26

Win, lose, or draw
Fight and give all you can give
Sometimes the winners
Are the ones who just outlive

Wherein ye greatly rejoice, though now for a season, if need
be, ye are in heaviness through manifold temptations. That the
trial of your faith, being much more precious than of gold that
perisheth, though it be tried with fire, might be found unto
praise and honour and glory at the appearing of Jesus Christ.

1 Peter 1:6, 7

Our blessings won't stop us from sometimes bleeding.

And the brother shall deliver up brother to death,
and the father the child: and the children shall rise up
against their parents, and cause them to be put to death.
And ye shall be hated of all men for my name's sake:
but he that endureth to the end shall be saved.

Matthew 10:21, 22

Judases have assignments too
That they perform fairly well
Betrayal is as necessary as loyalty
Even though the betrayed goes through a psychological hell

But as for you, ye thought evil against me; but
God meant it unto good, to bring to pass, as
it is this day, to save much people alive.

Genesis 50:20

There is a message in each moronic mess.

And the Word was made flesh, and dwelt among us,
(and we beheld his glory, the glory as of the only
begotten of the Father) full of grace and truth.

John 1:14

What you call empty
I call full
When you say push
I say pull

For the weapons of our warfare are not carnal, but might
through God to the pulling down of strongholds. Casting
down imaginations, and every high thing that exalted
itself against the knowledge of God, and bringing into
captivity every thought to the obedience of Christ.

2 Corinthians 10:4, 5

Canst thou hinder the heart or hand of God?

August 29

And the Lord said unto to Satan, Whence comest thou?
Then Satan answered the Lord, and said, From going to
and fro the earth, and from walking up and down in it.

Job 1:7

The Enemy's tentacles are always extended
Wrecking havoc untold
But the Truth is our light and buckler
Sacred secrets He'll surely unfold

But the Comforter, which is the Holy Ghost, whom the Father
will send in my name, he shall teach you all things, and bring
all things to your remembrance, whatsoever I have said to you.

John 14:26

Find and seek but don't believe what the Enemy speaks.

August 30

In all their affliction he was afflicted, and the angel of his presence saved them: in his love and in his pity he redeemed them; and he bare them, and carried them all the days of old.

Isaiah 63:9

Trouble is no doubt troublesome
It helps us grow and mature
Our test isn't the trouble itself
But how well we recall and endure

Though the mountains be shaken and the hills be removed, yet my unfailing love for you will not be shaken nor my covenant of peace be removed, says the Lord, who has compassion on you.

Isaiah 54:10

It is good that I have been afflicted that I might learn your statutes.

If my people, which are called by my name, shall humble themselves, and pray, and seek my face, and turn from their wicked ways; the will I hear from heaven, and will forgive their sin, and will heal their land.

2 Chronicles 7:14

IF represents our covenant
That will lead us to the depth of our destiny
Our heart desires will come to fruition
Within the circle of His reciprocity

And all these blessings shall come on thee, and overtake thee, if thou shalt hearken unto the voice of the Lord thy God. Blessed shalt thou be in the city, and blessed shalt thou be in the field. Blessed shalt thou be when thou comest in, and blessed shalt thou be when thou goest out.

Deuteronomy 28:2, 3, 6

Obedience enlarges our territory and adds a refreshing savor to our story.

September 1

I call heaven and earth to record this day against you, that
I have set before you life and death, blessing and cursing:
therefore choose life, that both thou and thy seed may live.
That thou mayest love the Lord thy God, and that thou
mayest obey his voice, and that thou mayest cleave unto
him: for he is thy life, and the length of thy days: that thou
mayest dwell in the land which the Lord sware unto thy
fathers, to Abraham, to Issac, and to Jacob to give them.

Deuteronomy 30:19, 20

It's a matter of priority
That we alone choose
But in order to win
We must first be willing to lose

He must increase; I must decrease.

John 3:30

Flip the Script and let the Word do the work.

Be not thou envious against evil men, neither
desire to be with them. For their heart studieth
destruction, and their lips talk of mischief.

Proverbs 24:1, 2

Envy and jealousy are tricks
Commit yourself to your charge
Diversity is within our individuality
And within is our capacity to live exceptionally large

Beloved, I wish above all things that thou mayest prosper
and be in health, even as thy soul prospereth.

3 John 2

Authenticity is better than multiplicity.

September 3

My doctrine shall drop as the rain, my speech shall
distill as dew, as the small rain upon the tender
herb, and as the showers upon the grass.

Deuteronomy 32:2

Grass doesn't grow
Without sunshine and rain
And trust muscles aren't developed
Without heartache and strain

He keepeth back his soul from the pit, and his life from
perishing by the sword. He is chastened also with pain upon
his bed, and the multitude of his bones with strong pain.

Job 33:18, 19

No pain, no gain.

And they told him, and said, We came unto the land whither thou sentest us, and surely it floweth with milk and honey; and this is the fruit of it. Nevertheless the people be strong that dwell in the land, and the cities are walled, and very great: and moreover we saw the children of Anak there.

Numbers 13:27, 28

Unnoticeables are not notable
Significant they are not
Our sustenance is in the substantial
And peripherals are just a part of the plot

And Caleb stilled the people before Moses, and said, Let us go up at once, and possess it; for we are well able to overcome it.

Numbers 13:30

Nothing substantial concedes without a demand.

September 5

Give us this day our daily bread.

Matthew 6:11

Our guiding force stands ready
So follow its prompting and lead
Other voices will clamor for our attention too
But be consciously aware and take heed

But he that entered in by the door is the shepherd of the sheep.
To him the porter openeth; and the sheep hear his voice: and
he calleth his own sheep by name, and leadeth them out.

John 10:2, 3

Where God guides, He also provides. Where He leads, He
feeds. And those whom He will reach, are also those whom He
will teach.

Christina Abby

September 6

And Jesus said unto him, No man, having put his hand to the plough, and looking back, is fit for the kingdom of God.

Luke 9:62

Stand in your conviction
Be firm and don't bend
Know that the enemy of the Enemy
Is foremost our closest friend

A friend loveth at all times, and a brother is born for adversity.

Proverbs 17:17

Here I am, send me.

September 7

The disciple is not above his master, but everyone that is perfect shall be as his master.

When you say have
I say be
What you assess costly
I attest to be free

Now we have received, not the spirit of the world,
but the spirit which is of God; that we might know
the things that are freely given to us of God.

1 Corinthians 2:12

For in Him we live, move, and have our being.

September 8

And one cried unto another and said, Holy, holy, holy, is the Lord of hosts: the whole earth is full of his glory. Then said I, Woe is me! For I am undone; because I am a man of unclean lips, and I dwell in the midst of a people of unclean lips: for mine eyes have seen the king, the Lord of hosts.

Isaiah 6:3, 5

Humble yourself in His presence
To satisfy your soul's thirst
Give Him the honor and glory due His name
For His adoration always comes first

Whether therefore ye eat, or drink, or whatsoever ye do, do all to the glory of God.

1 Corinthians 10:31

Our honor is wholly tied up in our humility.

September 9

He sent his word, and healed them, and delivered them from their destructions.

Psalm 107:20

O Lord of the heavens
We don't need very much
A Word from you would be sufficient
But our preference would be Your touch

And Jesus, immediately knowing in himself that virtue had
gone out of him, turned him about in the press, and said,
Who touched my clothes? And his disciples said unto him,
Thou seest the multitude thronging thee, and sayest thou, Who
touched me? And he said unto her, Daughter, thy faith hath
made thee whole; go in peace, and be whole of thy plague.

Mark 5:30, 31, 34

He loves each one of us as though there was but one of us.

Pure religion and undefiled before God and the Father
is this: To visit the fatherless and widows in their affliction, and to keep himself unspotted from the world.

James 1:27

What's the effectiveness of your life?
Comparatively, how would you rate?
If you scored perfectly
Then pride is residing at your estate

For they that are such serve not our Lord Jesus
Christ, but their own belly; and by good words and
fair speeches deceive the hearts of the simple.

Romans 16:18

If the hitch hiker displays his pride, pass him and don't dare let
him ride.

September 11

Wait on the Lord: be of good courage, and he shall
strengthen thine heart; wait, I say, on the Lord.

Psalm 27:14

Evildoers don't get away
Just give time appropriate room
They'll implode from the inside out
And we'll all see their doom

When Jesus therefore had received the vinegar, he said, It is
finished: and he bowed his head, and gave up the ghost.

John 19:30

Bye and bye, Lord, when the morning comes.

September 12

Then the Lord opened the eyes of Ba-laam, and he saw the
angel of the Lord standing in the way, and his sword drawn
in his hand: and he bowed down his head; and fell flat on his
face. And the angel of the Lord said unto him, Wherefore hast
thou smitten thine ass these three times? Behold, I went out
to withstand thee, because thy way is perverse before me.

Numbers 22:31, 32

Other gods can't compete
And are left motionless and mute
Our God is bigger and better
Hands down, He has no substitute

That in blessing I will bless thee, and in multiply-
ing I will multiply thy seed as the stars of the heaven,
and as the sand which is upon the sea shore; and
thy seed shall possess the gate of his enemies.

Genesis 22:17

Our God is mighty to save; He's mighty to save.

September 13

A man's gift maketh room for him, and bringeth him before great men.

Proverbs 18:16

Face the facts
Our critics won't ever be appeased
So be the sermon you want to see
Then both you and God can be pleased

I love them that love me; and those that
seek me early shall find me.

Proverbs 8:17

A souled-out soul can never be bought.

A man's pride shall bring him low; but honour
shall uphold the humble in spirit.

Proverbs 29:23

When you say simple
I say profound
What you call the cross
I call the crown

Ought not Christ to have suffered these
things and to enter into his glory?

Luke 24:26

Free at last, free at last. Thank God Almighty, we're free at last!

September 15

Because my people hath forgotten me, they have burned incense to vanity, and they have caused them to stumble in their ways from the ancient paths, to walk in paths, in a way not cast up. To make their land desolate, and a perpetual hissing; every one that passeth thereby shall be astonished and wag his head.

Jeremiah 18:15, 16

Made as image-bearers
With an innate sense of decency
What, what has happened to us?
Where is our dignity, respect, integrity?

He said unto them, An enemy hath done this. The servants said unto him, Wilt thou then that we go and gather them up? But he said, Nay; lest while ye gather up the tares, ye root up also the wheat with them.

Matthew 13:28, 29

And the Enemy shall be crushed under His feet shortly.

How precious also are thy thoughts unto me O God! How
great is the sum of them! If I should count them, they are more
in number than the sand; when I awake I am still with thee.

Psalm 139:17, 18

It takes no effort to render praise
When things are going well
But how faithful are those efforts
When our lives are languishing in hell

And at midnight Paul and Silas prayed, and sang praises
unto God; and the prisoners heard them. And suddenly
there was a great earthquake, so that the foundations of
the prison were shaken; and immediately all the doors
were opened, and everyone's bands were loosed.

Acts 16:25, 26

He's an on time God. Yes He is.

September 17

Boast not against the branches. But if thou boast,
thou bearest not the root, but the root thee.

Romans 11:18

Never profess to know much
Especially another's situation
A mind stayed on Jesus
Eliminates our own confusion and fragmentation

Thou wilt keep him in perfect peace, whose mind
is stayed on thee: because he trusteth in thee.

Isaiah 26:3

Your blues ain't my blues, but it doesn't mean I ain't got no blues.

The tongue of the wise useth knowledge aright: but
the mouth of fools poureth out foolishness.

Proverbs 15:2

Not responsible for others' behavior
Its our own we should regulate
When we wear the white hat in all our dealings
We can't ever transform into what we hate

Even a fool, when he holdeth his peace, is counted wise; and
he that shutteth his lips is esteemed a man of understanding.

Proverbs 17:28

Understanding is mellow.

September 19

In all labour there is profit: but the talk of
the lips tendeth only to penury.

Proverbs 14:23

When we get too comfortable
He's got to nudge and meddle
His desire is that reach higher
And He refuses to allow us to just settle

Go to the ant, thou sluggard; consider her ways, and be wise:
which having no guide, overseer, or ruler, provideth her
meat in the summer, and gathereth her food in the harvest.

Proverbs 6:6, 7, 8

God is more concerned about our character than our comfort.

September 20

To me belongeth vengeance, and recompence; their foot shall
slide in due time; for the day of their calamity is at hand,
and the things that shall come upon them make haste.

Vengeance is His
And in Him do we trust
Our response should be tailored and tempered
In His love which is both true and just

For therein is the righteousness of God revealed from
faith to faith, as it is written, The just shall live by faith.

Romans 1:17

A false balance is an abomination to the Lord; but a just weight
is His delight.

I have not written unto you because ye know not the truth,
but because ye know it, and that no lie is of the truth.

1 John 2:21

What you think is a lie
I know to be true
When you say how
I say WHO

And God said unto Moses, I AM THAT I AM, and he said
Thou shalt say unto the children of Israel, I AM hath sent me.

Exodus 3:14

The Rose of Sharon; The Lily of the Valley; The Bright
Morning Star.

September 22

Behold, I send you forth as sheep in the midst of wolves;
be ye therefore wise as serpents, and harmless as doves.

Matthew 10:16

Integrity connotes influence
Influence garners respect
When integrity is lacking
So is its influence and effect

Let your light so shine before me, that they may see your
good works, and glorify your Father which is in heaven.

Matthew 5:16

Tell the Truth and shame the devil.

September 23

But a certain Samaritan as he journeyed, came where he was, and when he saw him, he had compassion on him.

Luke 10:33

Share another's burdens
Young, old, damsel or dude
There's nothing less hollow
Than empty, pious platitudes

I have shewed you all things, how that so laboring ye ought to support the weak, and to remember the words of the Lord Jesus, how he said, It is more blessed to give than receive.

Acts 20:35

Higher risks translate into higher rewards.

September 24

And it was about the sixth hour, and there was darkness over all the earth until the ninth hour. And the sun was darkened, and the veil of the temple was rent in the midst.

Access has been granted
With a ransom of costly pain
The Enemy has been defeated
Now is the time to Reign. Reign. Reign

And I saw an angel come down from heaven, having the key of the bottomless pit and a great chain in his hand. And he laid hold on the dragon, that old serpent, which is the Devil, and Satan, and bound him a thousand years.

Revelation 20:1, 2

Get in where you fit in and claim your clout or be left out.

September 25

And he said unto them, I beheld Satan
as lightning fall from heaven.

Luke 10:18

It is finished!
The war has been won
The Enemy would like us to think and act otherwise
But he's already done

But he turned, and said unto Peter, Get thee behind me,
Satan: thou art an offence unto me for thou savourest not
the things that be of God, but those that be of men.

Matthew 16:23

Be careful in majoring in the minor and minoring in the major.

But there is forgiveness with thee, that thou mayest be feared. I
wait for the Lord, my soul doth wait, and in his word do I hope.

Psalm 130:4, 5

Forgiveness can be instantaneous
But restoration takes a bit of time
Revenge is counterproductive to the process
And everything afterwards isn't necessarily fine

And Jesus answered and said unto them, Elias truly
shall first come, and restore all things. But I say unto
you that Elias is come already, and they knew him
not, but have done unto him whatsoever they listed.
Likewise shall also the Son of man suffer of them.

Matthew 17:11, 12

Forgiveness imparts freedom to both the victim and the villain.

September 27

And David danced before the Lord with all his might;
and David was girded with a linen ephod. So David and
all the house of Israel brought up the ark of the Lord
with shouting, and with the sound of the trumpet.

2 Samuel 6:14, 15

Move forward
Rejoice, sing, and dance
Though you might have messed up this morning
Its afternoon so you have another chance

Blessed is he whose transgression is forgiven, whose
sin is covered. Blessed is the man unto whom the Lord
imputeth no iniquity, and in whose spirit is no guile.

Psalm 32:1, 2

Repent, reconcile, and remember.

September 28

So David prevailed over the Philistines with a sling
and with a stone, and smote the Philistine, and slew
him; but there was no sword in the hand of David.

1 Samuel 17:50

When you say small
I say big
What you call your life
I call your gig

For so hath the Lord commanded us, saying, I have set
thee to be a light of the Gentiles, that thou shouldest be for salvation unto the ends of the earth.

Acts 13:47

Dynamite is wrapped in small, unassuming packages.

September 29

And unto Adam he said, Because thou has hear-
kened unto the voice of thy wife, and hast eaten of
the tree, of which I commanded thee saying, Thou
shalt not eat of it; cursed is the ground for thy sake, in
sorrow shalt thou eat of it all the days of thy life.

Genesis 3:17

We're all in a fallen state
Relegated to a journey of struggle and strife
Thankfully, death isn't our final destination
BUT a transition into eternal life

It is sown in a natural body; it is raised spiritual body.
There is a natural body, and there is a spiritual body.
And so it is written, Then first man Adam was made a
living soul; the last Adam was mad a quickening spirit.

1 Corinthians 15:44, 45

O death, where is thy sting? O grave, where is thy victory?

September 30

Be not deceived; evil communications corrupt good manners.

1 Corinthians 15:33

Malicious gossip is poisonous
Any contribution gives it traction
If it were your character being assassinated
What would be your personal reaction?

He that goeth about as a talebearer revealeth secrets; therefore meddle not with him that flattereth with his lips.

Proverbs 20:19

The dog that brings a bone more often than not carries one also.

October 1

Whoso offereth praise glorifieth me: and to him that ordered
his conversation aright will I shew the salvation of God.

Are you fractured and frayed?
Well, the remedy is rather odd
If you really want to change your position
Just start worshiping and praising God

And at midnight Paul and Silas prayed and sang praises
unto God: and the prisoners heard them. And suddenly
there was a great earthquake, so that the foundations of
the prison were shaken: and immediately all the doors
were opened, and every one's bands were loosed.

Acts 16:25, 26

When praises go up, strongholds come down.

October 2

Blessed are the pure in heart; for they shall see God.

Matthew 5:8

First things first
Internalize and emulate
Think about how far you've come
And give thanks and celebrate

From the rising of the sun onto the going down
of the same the Lord's name is to be praised.

Psalm 113:3

I can think myself happy.

October 3

The words of his mouth were smoother than
butter, but war was in his heart: his words were
softer than oil, yet were they drawn swords.

Psalm 55:21

Be gracious and never ruthless
Treat everyone with respect
For our sins will surely find us out
When we least want and/or expect

But Peter said, Ananias, why hath Satan filled thine heart
to lie to the Holy Ghost, and to keep back part of the
price of the land? Then Peter said unto her, How is it
that ye have agreed together to tempt the Spirit of the
Lord? Behold, the feet of them which have buried thy
husband are at the door, and shall carry thee out.

Acts 5:3, 9

Be not deceived, God is never mocked.

286 | Christina Aobu

October 4

I form the light, and create darkness; I make peace,
and create evil; I the Lord do all these things.

Problems aren't random
Neither are they mistakes
Opposition is really an opportunity
To show Himself grand and great

And these three men, Shadrach, Meshach and Abednego
fell down bound into the midst of the burning fiery
furnace. He answered and said, Lo, I see four men loose,
walking in the midst of the fire, and they have no hurt;
and the form of the fourth is like the Son of God.

Daniel 3:23, 25

TRUTH is our buckler and His arc always bends toward justice.

October 5

And when he was in affliction, he besought the Lord his God,
and humbled himself greatly before the God of his fathers.
And prayed unto him; and he was intreated of him, and heard
his supplication and brought him again to Jerusalem into his
kingdom. Then Manasseh knew that the Lord was his God.

2 Chronicles 33:12, 13

Trials and adversity are par for the journey
And more instructive than what we can preach
The suffering associated with these lesson plans
Are the most effective vehicles with which to teach

My brethren, count it all joy when ye fall into divers
temptations; knowing this, that the trying of your faith
worketh patience. But let patience have her perfect work,
that ye may be perfect and entire, wanting nothing.

James 1:2, 3, 4

Our real conflict is between the Truth and the liar.

October 6

And now it came to pass on a certain day, that he went into a ship with his disciples; and he said unto them, Let us go over unto the other side of the lake. And they launched forth.

Luke 8:22

The beauty seen now
Will prove significantly pale
When we reach the other side
And realize we've done very well

His lord said unto him, Well done thou good and faithful servant; thou hast been faithful over a few things, I will make thee ruler over many things, enter thou into the joy of the Lord.

Matthew 25:21

Beneath the veneer of the illusion is the Truth and the final conclusion.

October 7

And he put forth his hand, and touched him, saying I will: be thou clean. And immediately the leprosy departed from him.

Luke 5:13

When you say filthy
I say clean
What you call barren
I call green

God setteth the solitary in families; he bringeth out those which are bound with chains, but the rebellious dwell in dry land.

Psalm 68:6

Think and act as though you are and you will be.

October 8

O bless our God, ye people, and make
the voice of his praise be heard.

Psalm 66:8

Praise summons Presence
Ingratitude drives it away
So would you rather your help-meet be nearby
Or kept limited and at bay

How shall I pardon thee for this? Thy children have forsaken me, and sworn by them that are no gods; when I had
fed them to the full, they then committed adultery, and
assembled themselves by troops in the harlots' houses.

Jeremiah 5:7

You'll never get the yacht if you decline to row the boat
you've got.

October 9

And Samuel said unto Jesse, Are here all thy children? And
he said, There remaineth yet the youngest, and, behold, he
keepeth the sheep. And Samuel said unto Jesse, Send and
fetch him: fore we will not sit down till he come hither.

1 Samuel 16:11

We are not what we do
Therefore, a job does not our identity define
Though one could be an NBA player
He/she could still be riding the pine

And she conceived, and bare a son; and said, God hath
taken away my reproach; And she called his name Joseph;
and said, the Lord shall add to me another son.

Genesis 30:23, 25

"I formed thee and you are Mine."

October 10

But call to remembrance the former days, in which, after ye were illuminated, ye endured a great fight of afflictions.

Hebrews 10:32

Don't be dismayed
Its just a temporary season
Into each life some rain must fall
And for every challenge there's a reason

For ye have need of patience, that after ye have done the will of God, ye might receive the promise. For yet a little while, and he that shall come will come, and will not tarry.

Hebrews 10:37, 38

Spiritual growth is a must so He allows rain to fall on both the evil and the just.

October 11

And Jesus said unto the centurion, Go thy way; and
as thou hast believed, so be it done unto thee. And
his servant was healed in the selfsame hour.

Matthew 8:13

You'll never accomplish what you want
While believing its too late
So channel your energy toward achieving the goal
Visualize and take a great leap of faith

Through faith we understand that the worlds were
framed by the word of God, so that things which are
seen were not made of things which do appear.

Hebrews 11:3

Seeing first is the Enemy of believing first.

October 12

No man also having drunk old wine straightway
desireth new: for he saith, The old is better.

Luke 5:39

Old patterns and habits are stubborn
Extremely difficult to break
But avoidance is a barrier to overcoming
And worst are the excuses we tend to make

And he spake also a parable unto them: No man putteth
a piece of a new garment upon an old; if otherwise,
then both the new maketh a rent, and the piece that
was taken out of the new agreeth not with the old.

Luke 5:36

Change is necessarily uncomfortable and unsettling due to
its uncertainty.

October 13

According as he hath chosen us in him before the
foundation of the world, that we should be holy and
without blame before him in love. Having predestinated
us unto the adoption of children by Jesus Christ to
himself, according to the good pleasure of his will.

Ephesians 1:4, 5

Our destination is in our destiny
The place where purpose is found
Where Truth is our demonstration
And where love, grace, and mercy abound

And the Word was made flesh, and dwelt among us,
(as we beheld his glory, the glory as of the only begotten of the Father) full of grace and truth.

John 1:14

And the two became One.

October 14

It is good for me that I have been afflicted
that I might learn thy statutes.

When you say wrong
I say right
When you say midnight
I say daylight

For his anger endureth but a moment; in
his favour is life: weeping may endure for a
night, but joy cometh in the morning.

Psalm 30:5

Our darkest hour is right before our dawn.

October 15

Buy the truth and sell it not; also wisdom,
instruction and understanding.

Proverbs 23:23

Glitter and glam
And the myriad products money can buy
Can't beautify or fulfill the longing
That only God can satisfy

For what is a man profited, if shall gain the
whole world, and lose his own soul? Or what
shall a man give in exchange for his soul?

Matthew 16:26

Pretty is what pretty does and a hollow soul is pretty ugly.

October 16

Be still before the Lord and wait patiently for
him; do not fret when men succeed in their ways,
when they carry out their wicked schemes.

Psalm 37:7

Truth will prevail
Whenever, however, wherever and why
Patience is trust in work clothes
So agree with God and continue to occupy

Can two walk together, except they be agreed?

Amos 3:3

Remember. The Enemy has been defeated.

October 17

He that hideth hatred with lying lips, and
he that uttereth a slander, is a fool.

Proverbs 10:18

Don't get caught up in foolishness
You'll invariably pay a fee
The toll will be expensive too
So ignore, hear or be what you wish to see

Be not deceived: God is not mocked; for whatsoever a man
soweth, that shall he also reap. For he that soweth to his
flesh shall of the flesh reap corruption; but he that soweth
to the Spirit shall of the Spirit reap life everlasting.

Galatians 6:7, 8

See no evil. Hear no evil. Speak no evil.

October 18

Ye have not chosen me, but I have chosen you, and
ordained you, that ye should go and bring forth fruit, and
that your fruit should remain: that whatsoever ye shall
ask of the Father in my name, he may give to you.

John 15:16

In His kingdom
No one is left out
Neither is there favoritism
Everybody's equally significant and has clout

Boast not against the branches. But if thou boast,
thou bearest not the root, but the root thee.

Romans 11:18

Any and all things good find their Source in the kingdom
of God.

October 19

But he himself went a day's journey into the wilderness, and came and sat down under a juniper tree: and he requested for himself that he might die and said: It is enough; now. O Lord, take away my life; for I am not better than my fathers.

1 Kings 19:4

Circumstances evolve rapidly
From tranquil to tragic
And when suddenly happens
Misery immediately transforms into magic

And suddenly there was a great earthquake, so that the foundations of the prison were shaken; and immediately all the doors were opened, and every one's bands were loosed.

Acts 16:26

Suddenly He shows up and immediately He shows out.

October 20

And if a kingdom be divided against itself, that
kingdom cannot stand. And if a house is divided
against itself, that house cannot stand.

Mark 3:24, 25

Divide and conquer
Like prostitution, its just an old trick
When the Enemy can't win meritoriously
He'll throw any and everything to see what sticks

And no marvel: for Satan himself is transformed into an angel of light.

2 Corinthians 11:14

Listening to and repeating a lie long enough will cause you to
believe and act like its true.

October 21

And a man that hath friends must shew himself friendly;
and there is a friend that sticketh closer than a brother.

Proverbs 18:24

When you say far
I say near
What you call procrastination
I call fear

For God hath not given us the spirit of fear, but
of power, and of love, and of a sound mind.

2 Timothy 1:7

Why are you so fearful?

October 22

Hath the rain a father? Or who hath begotten the
drops of dew? Out of whose womb came the ice? And
the hoary frost of heaven, who hath gendered it?

Job 38:28, 29

Pay attention to detail
There's majesty in sight and sound
The mundane is wonderfully orchestrated
Simple, but poignantly profound

But now, O Lord, thou art our father; we are the clay, and
thou our potter; and we are the work of thy hand.

Isaiah 64:8

The grand Architect of the universe painted the heavens
into existence.

Slothfulness casteth into a deep sleep, and
an idle soul shall suffer hunger.

Proverbs 19:15

Slothfulness, complacency, mediocrity
The destructive triple threats
Squandering and squashing dreams and destiny
And leaving the vestiges of lives lived in regret

The hand of the diligent shall bear rule but
the slothful shall be under tribute.

Proverbs 12:24

Idle hands, hearts, and heads are the Enemy's workshop.

October 24

The Lord replied, My Presence will go
with you, and I will give you rest.

Exodus 33:14

In a dry season
Don't know where you're going
Well, you're exactly where He wants you to be
For needing Him is actually knowing

The secret of the Lord is with them that fear him, and he
will shew them his covenant. Mine eyes are ever toward
the Lord, for he shall pluck my feet out of the net.

Psalm 25:14, 15

The mystery of His power can't be adequately explained or told
BUT His glory has always remained.

October 25

A man's steps are directed by the Lord. How
then can anyone understand his own way.

Teach us, Lord
Your Will, Your Wisdom, Your Way
Gird, guide, and instruct us
In all we should do, be, and say

I will instruct thee and teach thee in the way which
thou shalt go; I will guide thee with mine eye.

Psalm 32:8

Focus on the Presence rather than the problem.

298 | Christina Abby

October 26

I am the good shepherd: the good shepherd giveth his life for the sheep.

John 10:11

Have confidence in His goodness
His people doth He adore
His leadership is unparalleled and unfailing
And on none will He shut the door

Come unto me all that labour and are heavy
laden and I will give you rest.

Matthew 11:28

The door to the Church is open.

To every thing there is a season, and a time to every purpose
under the heaven. A time to be born, and a time to die; a
time to plant, and a time to pluck up that which is planted.

Ecclesiastes 3:1, 2

Timing is everything
Manifold dimensions has He revealed
All things come to pass in their due season
And nothing can be stymied or concealed

And he shall be like a tree planted by the rivers
of water, that bringeth forth his fruit in his
season; his leaf also shall not wither.

Psalm 1:3

Now the parable is this: The seed is the word of God.

And he said, So is the kingdom of God as if a man should cast
seed unto the ground. And should sleep, and rise night and day,
and the seed should spring and grow up, he knoweth not how.

Mark 4:26, 27

When you say ebb
I say flow
When you say above
I say below also

I had fainted unless I had believed to see the goodness of the Lord in the land of the living. Wait
on the Lord; be of good courage and he shall
strengthen thine heart. Wait, I say, on the Lord.

Psalm 27:13, 14

Heaven and earth are states of consciousness.

October 29

Fret not thyself because of evildoers, neither be
thou envious against workers of iniquity.

It aint over until its over
There's no need to frown or fret
The Script is aptly Flippin'
So don't give up just yet

Persecutions, afflictions, which came unto me at
Antioch, at Iconium at Lystra; what persecutions I
endured; but of them all the Lord delivered me.

2 Timothy 3:11

Flip the Script and let the Word do the work.

He giveth power to the faint; and to them that
have no might he increaseth strength.

Isaiah 40:29

The power is yours
So don't play the fool
Meekness is strength under control
Calm, collected, and cool

The meek shall eat and be satisfied; they shall praise the
Lord that seek him; your heart shall live forever.

Psalm 22:26

Not by power nor by might, but by His Spirit.

October 31

My heart was hot within me, while I was musing
the fire burned; then spake I with my tongue.

Psalm 39:3

An encounter with the Divine
Is like an all-encompassing fire
A change happens instantaneously
Then worship becomes our natural desire

For the Lord thy God is a consuming fire, even as jealous God.

Deuteronomy 4:24

Take away the dross from the silver and it goes to the silversmith
as jewelry.

These things I have spoken unto you, that in me ye
might have peace. In the world ye shall have tribulation;
but be of good cheer; I have overcome the world.

John 16:33

Failure is not an option
When passion and destiny collide
Its all just a matter of time
For the victory is already on our side

For whatsoever is born of God overcometh the world:
and this is the victory that overcometh the world, even
our faith. Who is he that overcometh the world, but
he that believeth that Jesus is the Son of God.

1 John 5:4, 5

Winners never quit and quitters never win.

November 2

For whosever hath, to him shall be given, and he
shall have more abundance: but whosoever hath not,
from him shall be taken away even that he hath.

Matthew 13:12

Houses, cars, people
What would you be willing to sacrifice?
If you could acquire unlimited treasure
Would you choose the pearl of great price?

Again, the kingdom of heaven is like unto a merchant man
seeking goodly pearls: Who, when he had found one pearl
of great price, went and sold all that he had, and bought it.

Matthew 13:45, 46

Buy the Truth and do not sell it.

November 3

Then said I, Woe is me! For I am undone; because I am a man of unclean lips, and I dwell in the midst of a people of unclean lips: for mine eyes have seen the King, the Lord of hosts.

Isaiah 6:5

A vision pierces the heart
And exposes the magnitude of our guilt
While revelation is painfully frustrating
Its at this crossroad that our lives are rebuilt

Come now, and let us reason together, saith the Lord, though your sins be as scarlet, they shall be as white as snow; though they be red like crimson, they shall be as wool.

Isaiah 1:18

Our best days are not behind us but before us.

November 4

Then spake Jesus unto them, saying, I am the light
of the world: he that followeth me shall not walk
in darkness, but shall have the light of life.

John 8:12

Truth is the light
In darkness lurks the lie
And it will metastasize and consume itself
Leaving the liar questioning why

I have not written unto you because ye know not the
truth, but because ye know it, and that no lie is in the
truth. Who is a liar but he that denieth that Jesus is the
Christ? He is antichrist, and denieth the Father and Son.

1 John 2:21, 22

This little light of mine I'm gonna let it shine.

Where there is no vision, the people perish:
but he that keepeth the law, happy is he.

Proverbs 29:18

Pure unadulterated Truth
Is no meaningless blather
Some prefer it as it is
But others would rather…..

When the righteous are in authority, the people rejoice;
but when the wicked beareth rule, the people mourn.

Proverbs 29:2

Flip the Script and let the Word do the work.

November 6

But thou shalt remember the Lord thy God: for it is he that
giveth thee power to get wealth, that he may establish his
covenant which he sware unto thy fathers, as it is this day.

Deuteronomy 8:18

Its not all about the money
Nor the value of our material stuff
When we're connected to the Source
We'll always have more than just enough

The young lions do lack, and suffer hunger: but they
that seek the Lord shall not want any good thing.

Psalm 34:10

Make some money but don't let some money make you.

November 7

Verily, verily I say unto you, Except a corn of wheat fall into the ground and die, it abideth alone; but if it die, it bringeth forth much fruit. He that love his life shall lose it; and he that hateth his life in the world shall keep it unto life eternal.

John 12:24, 25

When you say subtraction
I say addition
What you call conversion
I call recognition

He answered and said, Whether he be a sinner or no, I know not; one thing I know that whereas I was blind, now I see.

John 9:25

Acknowledge. Accept. Surrender and die daily.

November 8

And, behold, I am with thee, and will keep thee in
all places whither thou goest, and will bring thee
again into this land; for I will not leave thee, until I
have done that which I have spoken to thee of.

Genesis 28:15

Full force ahead
You can accomplish anything
Though fear will try and stalk you
God will clamp to you and cling

And I will make of thee a great nation, and I will bless thee,
and make thy name great; and thou shalt be a blessing. And
I will bless them that bless thee, and curse him that curseth
thee: and in thee shall all families of the earth be blessed.

Genesis 12:2, 3

He's got the whole world in His hand.

November 9

But in mine adversity they rejoiced, and gathered themselves together: yea, the abjects gathered themselves together against me, and I knew it not; they did tear, and ceased not.

Running and hiding
In reality they're not really fine
They can choose now or later to surrender
But regardless the Light is gonna shine

And shalt say unto them, Thus saith the Lord of hosts; Even so will I break this people and this city, as one breaketh a potter's vessel, that cannot be made whole again: and they shall bury them in Tophet, till there be no place to bury.

Jeremiah 19:11

Don't worry. Be happy.

November 10

And Jabez was more honourable than his brethren: and his mother called his name Jabez,
saying, Because I bare him with sorrow.

1 Chronicles 4:9

Our journey is rarely linear
And not accomplished step by step
We may never fully understand
But our prayer should be to enlarge our concept

And Jabez called on the God of Israel, saying, Oh that
thou wouldest bless me indeed, and enlarge my coast,
and that thine hand might be with me, and thou wouldest keep me from evil, that it may not grieve me.
And God granted him that which he requested.

1 Chronicles 4:10

Don't give in, but pray and then get up.

November 11

For to be carnally minded is death; but to be
spiritually minded is life and peace.

Romans 8:6

Security is what we're seeking
When all our so called friends are gone
External things will elude us
Eternally, our redemption rest in Him alone

For we know that the whole creation groaneth
and travaileth in pain together unto now.

Romans 8:22

The kingdom is within and manifested without.

November 12

And Moses said unto the people, Fear ye not, stand still
and see the salvation of the Lord, which he will shew
to you today: for the Egyptians whom ye have seen
today, ye shall see them again no more forever.

Exodus 14:13

Be confident and courageous
We have the right and ability to stand
So squash the Enemy's chatter right now
Yes we can. Yes we can.

And Moses stretched out his hand over the sea; and the Lord
caused the sea to go back by a strong east wind all that night,
and made the sea dry land, and the waters were divided.

Exodus 14:21

If you don't stand for something, you'll fall for nothing.

November 13

For the thing which I greatly feared is come upon me, and
that which I was afraid of is come unto me. I was not in safety,
neither had I rest, neither was I quiet, yet trouble came.

Job 3:25, 26

Good God from Gulfport!
Will it ever end?
Practical problems have spiritual solutions
That end with an extreme makeover within

I have heard of thee by the hearing of the ear;
but now mine eye seeth thee. Wherefore I abhor
myself, and repent in dust and ashes.

Job 42:5, 6

Within the problem is its own solution just waiting to happen.

November 14

And he said, Woe unto you also, ye lawyers! For ye lade men with burdens grievous to be borne, and ye yourselves touch not the burdens with one of your fingers.

Luke 11:46

When you say cause
I say effect
What you call attentiveness
I call neglect

Woe unto you scribes and Pharisees, hypocrites. For ye pay tithes of mint and anise and cummin and have omitted the weightier matters of the law, judgment, mercy and faith: these ought ye to have done, and not leave the other undone.

Matthew 23:23

Our security and comfort lies in the Creator and not His creatures nor their creations.

Study to shew thyself approved unto God, a workman
that needeth not to be ashamed, rightly dividing the
word of truth. But shun profane and vain babblings
for they will increase unto more ungodliness.

2 Timothy 2:15, 16

Behavior is modified
By knowledge, force or fear
Our expectations are often crushed
When we fail to think, look, or hear

But that on good ground are they, which is an
honest and good heart, having heard the word,
keep it, and bring forth fruit with patience.

Luke 8:15

Flip the Script and let the Word do the work.

November 16

He will not suffer thy foot to be moved: he
that keepeth thee will not slumber.

Psalm 121:3

Simplicity and profundity are interwined
Its being wholly awake and fully aware
Without organicity of mind, body and soul
We'll never reach the destination called "there"

When thou liest down, thou shalt not be afraid: yea,
thou shalt lie down, and thy sleep shall be sweet.

Proverbs 3:24

Jesus wept.

November 17

And the Lord said unto him, Now do ye Pharisees make clean
the outside of the cup and the platter; but your inward part
is full of ravening and wickedness. Ye fools, did not he that
made that which is without make that which is within also?

Luke 11:39, 40

Time and energy are commodities
Irrelevancy is a distraction
Being right isn't necessarily righteous
We determine what we give any traction

Take heed that ye do not your alms before
men, to be seen of them: otherwise ye have no
reward of your Father which is in heaven.

Matthew 6:1

The greatest of all matter is to know what truly matters.

November 18

Again, the kingdom of heaven is like unto a merchant man,
seeking goodly pearls: Who, when had found one pearl of
great price, went and sold all that he had, and bought it.

Quality over quantity
Absolutely a must
Little is much when God is in it
Treasures acquired reflect a progression of trust

Again, the kingdom of heaven is like unto treasure hid in a
field; which when a man hath found, he hideth, and for thereof
goeth and selleth all that he hath, and buyeth that field.

Matthew 13:44

Just keep digging in the mature and you'll find your prized pony.

322 | Christina Abby

November 19

Wait on the Lord: be of good courage; and he shall
strengthen thine heart: wait, I say, on the Lord.

Psalm 27:14

We may not know when
What, why or how
But faith isn't faith when we know it all
Bend, but don't bow

Be still, and know that I am God; I will be exalted
among the heathen, I will be exalted in the earth.

Psalm 46:10

Get in it and be in it to win it!

They know not, neither will they understand; they walk on in darkness; all the foundations of the earth are out of course.

Psalm 82:5

A stark comparison
And noticeable contrast
Characterless foundations
Won't ever succeed or ever last

But he that heareth, and doeth not, is like a man that without a foundation built an house upon the earth: against which the stream did beat vehemently, and immediately it fell; and the ruin of that house was great.

Luke 6:49

If the foundation be destroyed, what shall the righteous do?

Then Peter said, Silver and gold have I none;
but such as I have give I thee: In the name of
Jesus Christ of Nazareth, rise up and walk.

Acts 3:6

What you think is less
I know to be more
Whom you despise
I truly adore

For who maketh thee to differ from another? And what hast
thou that thou didst not receive? Now if thou didn't receive
it, why does thou glory, as if thou hadst not received it?

1 Corinthians 4:7

One man's trash is another man's treasure.

Brethren, I count not myself to have apprehended: but this one thing I do, forgetting those things which are behind, and reaching forth unto those things which are before. I press toward the mark for the prize of the high calling of God in Christ Jesus.

Philippians 3:13, 14

Sweep around your own front door
While you have opportunity and space
No one can do what you're born to do
All have an appointed time and place

And I said, What shall I do, Lord? And the Lord said unto me, Arise, and go into Damascus; and there it shall be told thee of all things which are appointed for thee to do.

Acts 22:10

When we can agree to disagree agreeably then we'll always be in agreement.

November 23

But they mocked the messengers of God, and despised his
words, and misused his prophets, until the wrath of the
Lord arose against his people, till there was not remedy.

2 Chronicles 36:16

Misuse or abuse of power
Is rooted in a self-serving philosophy
But justice determines, directs, dictates
And demands reciprocity

And they shall fight against thee; but they shall not prevail
against thee: for I am with thee, saith the Lord, to deliver thee.

Jeremiah 1:19

The fight has already been fixed.

November 24

I have sworn by myself, the word is gone out of my mouth in righteousness, and shall not return, that unto me every knee shall bow, every tongue shall swear.

Isaiah 45:23

Resistance is futile
There is an end to the story
Creation was made by and for the Creator
In and only for His glory

Declaring the end from the beginning, and from ancient times the things that are not yet done, saying, My counsel shall stand, and I will do all my pleasures.

Isaiah 46:10

Besides Him there is none else.

November 25

To every thing there is a season, and time in every purpose
under the heaven: A time to be born, and a time to die; a
time to plant, and a time to pluck up that which is planted.

Ecclesiastes 3:1, 2

Timing is everything
Not a second, minute, hour too early or late
Desire and destiny will collide and coalesce
But the reality is that we all have to wait

If a man die, shall he live again? All the days of my
appointed time will I wait, till my change come.

Job 14:14

Timing is the only gnawing dictator that requires time to appease.

November 26

Jesus said unto him, If thou canst believe, all
things are possible to him that believeth.

Mark 9:23

Within the problems is its own solution
Has been since all creation
Recognition of this Truth
Is one of the greatest forms of illumination

Arise, shine; for thy light is come, and the glory of the Lord
is risen upon thee. For, behold, the darkness shall cover
the earth, and gross darkness the people; but the Lord shall
arise upon thee, and his glory shall be seen upon thee.

Isaiah 60:1, 2

We have to be readied for prime time.

Sing praises to the Lord, which dwelleth in Zion;
declare among the people his doings.

Psalm 9:11

It's the defining moment
After all has been said and done
You're in the best place you could be
Now call 9:11

And the people, when they knew it followed him: and
he received them and spake unto them of the kingdom
of God and healed them that had need of healing.

Luke 9:11

Our greatest opposition is our greatest opportunity.

Labour not for the meat which perisheth, but for that meat
which endureth unto everlasting life, which the Son of man
shall give unto you: for him hath God the Father sealed.

John 6:27

When you say first
I say last
What you call the future
I call the present and the past

And Jesus said unto him, Verily I say unto thee,
today shalt thou be with me in paradise.

Luke 23:43

Flip the Script and let the Word do the work.

November 29

A good man obtaineth favour of the Lord; but a
man of wicked devices will he condemn.

Proverbs 12:2

Buzzards and vultures
A disgustingly ravenous bunch
Like morally bankrupt human beings
Who crave position, status, and a free lunch

Better is little with fear of the Lord than
great treasure and trouble therewith.

Proverbs 15:16

There is none so blind as those who refuse to see that free isn't
always what its cooked up to be.

November 30

Come unto me, all ye that labour and are heavy laden, and I will give you rest. Take my yoke upon you, and learn of me; for I am meek and lowly in heart; and ye shall find rest unto your souls.

Matthew 11:28, 29, 30

Its not about prestige or power
Intimacy is enough
Seek a relationship with Him first
And along comes all the other stuff

But seek ye first the kingdom of God, and his righteousness; and all these things shall be added unto you.

Matthew 6:33

Those who do best are the ones who invest.

December 1

For we would not, brethren have you ignorant of our trouble which came to us in Asia, that were pressed out of measure, above strength, insomuch that we despised even of life. But we had the sentence of death in ourselves, that we should not trust ourselves, but in God which raised the dead.

2 Corinthians 1:8, 9

Take heart
Consider it not strange what's happening to you
Remember. Remember. Remember.
We all have to go through to get to

But and if ye suffer for righteousness sake, happy are ye: and be not afraid of their terror neither be troubled. But sanctify the Lord God in your hearts: and be ready always to give and answer to every man that asketh you a reason of the hope that is in you with meekness and fear.

1 Peter 4:14, 15

It is the crushing of the olive that produces the oil.

December 2

In everything give thanks: for this is the will
of God in Christ Jesus concerning you.

1 Thessalonians 5:18

Circumstances may appear impossibly bleak
But when its over and done
You'll thank the Enemy
For provoking your change to come

The righteous shall see it and rejoice; and all iniquity shall
stop their mouth. Whoso is wise, and will observe these things,
even they shall understand the lovingkindness of the Lord.

Psalm 107:43, 43

It may have happened to you, but it was really happening for you.

Woe unto you, scribes and Pharisees, hypocrites! For ye pay
tithe of mint and anise and cummin and have omitted the
weightier matters of the law, judgment, mercy and faith: these
ought ye have done and not to leave the other undone. Ye
blind guides which strain at a gnat; and swallow a camel.

Matthew 23:23, 24

Religion in its raw form
Isn't worth a hill of beans
While guilt and condemnation may evoke fear
Its end result doesn't justify the means

Woe unto you, scribes and Pharisees, hypocrites! For ye are like
unto whited sepulchers, which indeed appear beautiful outward,
but are within full of dead men's bones and of all uncleanness.

Matthew 23:27

The mirror reflects inwardly outwardly.

December 4

And Peter answered him and said, Lord if it be thou, bid me come unto thee on the water. And he said, Come. And when Peter was come down out of the ship, he walked on the water, to go to Jesus. But when he saw the wind boisterous, he was afraid; and beginning to sink, he cried, saying, Lord save me.

Matthew 14:28, 29, 30

We won't overcome our battles
When we focus entirely on our adversity
We're preparing ourselves for defeat
When we can't visualize our victory

And he said unto them, Where is your faith? And they being afraid, saying one to another, What manner of man is this! For he commandeth even the winds and water they obey him.

Luke 8:25

He who is not faithfully preparing to win has already prepared to lose.

December 5

And that he died for all, that they which live should
not henceforth live unto themselves, but unto
him which died for them and rose again.

2 Corinthians 5:15

There's no variation or partiality
The message of old still remains true
What was done for Job, Joseph, Solomon
Can be done for and through me and you

But as many as received him, to them gave he power to become
the sons of God, even to them that believe on his name.

John 1:12

If you can believe you can achieve.

December 6

And he spake many things unto them in parables, saying,
Behold a sower went forth to sow; Some fell upon stony
places, where they had not much earth: and forthwith
they sprung up, because they had no deepness of earth.

Matthew 13:3, 5

Shallow is least substantive
We've got to dig deep
As we sow, cultivate and prune
Likewise we shall also reap

But this I say, He which soweth sparingly shall
reap also sparingly; and he which soweth bountifully shall reap also bountifully.

2 Corinthians 9:6

We learn to maneuver the small spaces while cultivating and
pruning thoughts that lead to bigger places.

December 7

In the beginning God created the heaven and earth.

Genesis 1:1

When you say profound
I say simple
What you call a frown
I call a dimple

The Lord shall laugh at him for he sees that his day is coming.

Psalm 37:13

It's a comedy that life's a tragedy.

December 8

Pray without ceasing.

1 Thessalonians 5:17

Remain cognizant of your requests
Be careful in asking for a lot
The real question might end up being
Do you have capacity and commitment to handle it or not?

But he that knew not, and did commit things worthy of
stripes, shall be beaten with few stripes. For unto whomsoever
much is given, of him shall much be required; and to whom
men have committed much, of him they will ask the more.

Luke 12:48

Can you stand to be blessed?

December 9

And he humbled thee, and suffered thee to hunger, and
fed thee with manna, which thou knewest not, neither
did thy fathers know; that he might make thee know that
man doth not live by bread only but by every word that
proceedeth out of the mouth of the Lord doth man live.

Deuteronomy 8:3

There is none other like Him
Who can set His boundary and domain?
Idols are unacceptable
And therefore grossly profane

Beware lest any man spoil you through philosophy
and vain deceit, after the tradition of men, after the
rudiments of the world, and not after Christ.

Colossians 2:8

I AM the Way the Truth and Life.

December 10

But I say unto you, Love your enemies, bless them that
curse you, do good to them that hate you, and pray for
them which despitefully use you, and persecute you.

Matthew 5:44

People are rude and insensitive
And will verbally and physically attack
But life is just 10% of what happens to us
And 90% of how we react

Let your speech be always with grace, seasoned with salt,
that ye may know how we ought to answer every man.

Colossians 4:6

Change is inevitable, but growth is optional.

Where envy and self-seeking exist, confusion and every evil thing are there.

James 3:16

Hidden sin isn't unnoticed
Only a fool could wrongfully suppose
The Eyes have Eyes that we can't see
And they supernaturally will expose

For nothing is secret, that shall not be made manifest; neither
any thing hid, that shall not be known and come abroad.

Luke 8:17

Our sins will find us out.

December 12

Withhold not good from them to whom it is due,
when it is in the power of thine hand to do it. Say not
unto thy neighbor, Go, and come again and tomorrow I will give; when thou hast it by thee.

Proverbs 3:27, 28

Heartfelt desires are noble
Servanthood fosters spiritual elevation
Be cautious what you pray for
And be prepared for a period of isolation

Now the Lord had said unto Abram, Get thee out
of thy country, and from thy kindred, and from thy
fathers house, unto a land that I will shew thee.

Genesis 12:1

Entry into heaven isn't on a group rate basis but based on a personal relationship.

December 13

For the wages of sin is death; but the gift of God
is eternal life through Jesus Christ our Lord.

Romans 6:23

Bentley, Benz or bicycle
Each is a gift
Ungratefulness is sin
While gratitude provokes a conscious mind shift

Follow peace with all men, and holiness, without which
no man shall see the Lord. Looking diligently lest any
man fail of the grace of God; lest any root of bitterness
springing up trouble you, and thereby many be defiled.

Hebrews 12:14, 15

Our outlook determines our outcome.

December 14

The kingdom of God cometh without observa-
tion. Neither shall they say Lo here! Or lo there for
behold the kingdom of God is within you.

When you say out
I say in
What you call ignorance
I call the universal sin

And now brethren, I wot that through ignorance ye did it, as did also your rulers.

Acts 3:17

Be internally motivated rather than externally driven.

Decomber 15

And when he came to himself, he said, How many hired
servants of my fathers have bread enough and to spare, and I
perish with hunger! I will arise and go to my father, and will say
unto him, Father, I have sinned against heaven and before thee.

Luke 15:17, 18

Life happens
And sometimes spins out of control
Remember, we do have a disaster preparedness plan:
The reconnection to the Lover of our Soul

And he said unto him, Son thou art ever
with me, and all that I have is thine.

Luke 15:31

Our lives and times are in His hand.

December 16

Before I formed thee in the belly, I knew thee; and
before thou camest forth out of the womb I sanctified
thee, and I ordained thee a prophet unto the nations.

Jeremiah 1:5

To thine own self be true
No one apart from God knows you like you
Others will attempt to assign and define you
And you won't know who you are when they get through

What is man that thou art so mindful of him?
And the son of man, thou visitest him?

Psalm 8:4

Think and see yourself through His eyes and mind for He and
He alone has the authority to assign and define.

December 17

No man can serve two masters: for either he will hate the one, and love the other; or else he will hold to the one, and despise the other. Ye cannot serve God and mammon.

Matthew 6:24

The points have been tallied
The villain's total is a zero
Would you prefer being affiliated with a loser?
Or standing proud and tall with a Hero

And if it seem evil unto you to serve the Lord, choose you this day whom ye will serve; whether the gods which your fathers served that were on the other side of the flood, or the gods of the Amorites, in whose land ye dwell: but as for me and my house, we will serve the Lord.

Joshua 24:15

Flip the Script and let the Word do the work.

December 18

O Lord our Lord, how excellent is thy name in all the earth!

Psalm 8:9

Life is good
Blessings are meant to savor
Our gratitude is key to continuity
Thank God for His ongoing favor

The Lord hath made all things for himself; yea,
even the wicked for the day of evil.

Proverbs 16:4

We're close to our destination called there when we sense spiritually we're becoming aware.

December 19

For whom the Lord loveth he chasteneth, and
scourgeth every son who he receiveth.

Hebrews 12:6

Back at square one
Ain't learned the lesson yet?
Only a masochistic fool prefers a chastening rod
Forgive yourself, but don't ever forget

Now no chastening for the present seemeth to be joyous,
but grievous: nevertheless after it yieldeth the peaceable fruit
of righteousness unto them which are exercised by it.

Hebrews 12:11

Life is a journey of lessons learned and wisdom applied. When
you don't learn the lesson, you're apt to repeat the course.

For if thou altogether holdest thy peace at this time,
then shall there enlargement and deliverance arise to
the Jews from another place; but thou and thy father's
house shall be destroyed; and who knoweth whether
thou art come to the kingdom for such a time as this?

Esther 4:14

Lights, Camera, Action
Providence is working behind the scene
Though the plot thickens
The nightmare is vitally important to the dream

So they hanged Haman on the gallows that he had prepared for Mordecai. Then was the king's wrath pacified.

Esther 7:10

God has a way of turning things inside out and upside down.

December 21

For the bread of God is he which cometh down
from heaven and giveth life into the world.

John 6:33

When you say meat
I say bread
What you call the heart
I call the head

Let the words of my mouth and meditation of my heart be
acceptable in thy sight, O Lord, my strength and my redeemer.

Psalm 19:14

How can you meditate with your heart unless the consciousness
of the act resides in your head?

And he said, Unto you it is given to know the mysteries of
the kingdom of God; but to others in parables, that seeing
they might not see, and hearing they might not understand.

Luke 8:10

Pay attention to detail
Observe the beauty in sight and sound
There's a meticulously ordained universe
That is both simple and profound

And parable spake unto them: The kingdom of heaven
is like unto leaven, which a woman took, and hid in
three measures of meal, till the whole was leavened.

Matthew 13:33

Still waters run deep.

December 23

And the Lord said to Samuel, Behold, I will do a thing in Israel, at which both the ears of every one that heareth it shall tingle.

1 Samuel 3:11

You may expect Him at noon
But miracles also happen at night
When you think the solution is coming from the left
By golly, He shows up on the right

And after the earthquake a fire; but the Lord was not in the fire; and after the fire a still small voice, And it was so, when Elijah heard it, that he wrapped his face in his mantle, and went out, and stood in the entering in of the cave. And behold, there came a voice unto him, and said, What doest thou here, Elijah?

1 Kings 19:12, 13

For our God is in heaven and He does whatever He pleases.

December 24

Buy the truth, and sell it not; also wisdom,
and instruction, and understanding.

Proverbs 23:23

Money can buy a lot of things
But not peace of mind
People are more important than politics
What's more important to God than humankind?

Hereby perceive we the love of God, because he laid down
his life for us; and we ought to lay down our lives for the
brethren. But whoso hath this world's goods, and seeth
his brother have need, and shutteth his bowels of compassion from him, how dwelleth the love of God in him.

1 John 3:16, 17

Blessed to be a blessing.

For unto us a child is born, unto us a son is given: and the government shall be upon his shoulder: and his name shall be called Wonderful, Counsellor, Thy mighty God, The Everlasting Father, The Prince of Peace.

Isaiah 9:6

Celebrate Christmas daily
Sounds a little bizarre
Wise men understand the content and context
And constantly follows their guiding star

I Jesus have sent mine angel to testify unto you these things in the churches. I am the root and the off-spring of David, and bright and morning star.

Revelation 22:16

We can't beat God giving no matter how hard we try.

December 26

Study to shew thyself approved unto God, a workman that
needeth not be ashamed, rightly dividing the word of truth.

2 Timothy 2:15

We don't have to be genius
Or fanatically very bright
To understand that it is never ever wrong
To do whatever we know is right

Finally, brethren, whatsoever things are true, whatsoever things
are honest, whatsoever things are pure, whatsoever things are
lovely, whatsoever things are of good report; if there be any
virtue, and if there be any praise, think on these things.

Philippians 4:8

Do unto to others as you'd have them do unto you.

December 27

But if ye have bitter envying and strife in your hearts, glory not, and lie not against the truth. For where envying and strife is, there is confusion and every evil work.

James 4:14, 16

An overdose of self-importance
Makes us think we know what we really don't know
God shares His glory with no one
So our egos have to go

Yet thou shalt be brought down to hell, to the sides of the pit. They that see thee shall narrowly look upon thee, and consider thee, saying, Is this the man that made earth the tremble, that did shake kingdoms.

Isaiah 14:15, 16

Only the ego needs massaging; the Spirit just is.

December 28

Humble yourselves in the sight of the
Lord, and he shall lift you up.

James 4:10

When you say low
I say high
What you call the mind
I call the eye

The light of the body is the eye; therefore, when thine
eye is single thy whole body is full of light; but when
thine eye is evil, thy body also is full of darkness.

Luke 11:34

In the Mind's eye is the answer to the who, the what, the when
and the why.

December 29

Blessed is he whose transgression is forgiven, who sin is covered.

Psalm 32:1

Taste and see that the Lord is good
Who bestows blessings of all sizes and flavor
None of which we are entitled
Oh what unmerited favor

Come and hear, all ye that fear God, and I will
declare what he hath done for my soul.

Psalm 66:16

Favor is favor is favor.

December 30

For as he thinketh in his heart, so is he; Eat and drink,
saith he to thee, but his heart is not with thee.

Proverbs 23:7

Its easy to get it twisted
Our view and the kingdom's are worlds apart
Though the head may speak a language we want to hear
Its best to listen to and follow the heart

And they said one to another, Did not our heart
burn within us, while he talked with us by the
way and while opened to us the scriptures.

Luke 24:32

Listen and believe with all your heart instead and tame the tyrant
that's inside your head.

December 31

Therefore whosoever heareth these sayings of mine, and doeth them, I will liken him unto a wise man, which built his house upon a rock. And the rain descended, and the floods came, and the winds blew, and beat upon that house; and it fell not; for it was founded upon a rock.

Matthew 7:24, 25

What we trust today
Will fail the next
God is Faithful and True
Our fulfillment happens in the right context

And every one that heareth these sayings of mine, and doeth them not, shall be likened unto a foolish man, which built his house upon the sand. And the rain descended, and the floods came, and the winds blew, and beat upon that house; and it fell, and great was the fall of it.

Matthew 23:26, 27

Flip the Script and let the Word do the work.

3/P